F
into the Storm

Returning to face
childhood loss and
bereavement

Pete Armstrong

Copyright 2015 Pete Armstrong

All rights reserved

Find out more about Pete Armstrong
and read his blog about the inner journey at
www.holybloke.com

cover design: Rowan Swale

published by holybloke

About the Author

Pete Armstrong is a writer, poet, and guide to your inner journey.

Also available:

The Commitment of the Lark: poems for looking deeply

Target Practice: a guidebook of 100 poems and one song for your inner journey

Dedication

For my dad, Ernest Armstrong.

For all those who died early, and for all of us who grieve for them.

Please note: I have changed the names of a few individuals in the story where I was unable to contact them about the book.

For who knows what is just over the horizon

When, over the horizon,
Death drops in on someone we love
it creates a storm of grief.

When the storm reaches us
we are pounded and battered
by continual huge waves
that toss us about in the surf like a rag doll
so that we know we are dying too.

Later the energy subsides a little
and we are just waiting for the next big wave
to roll us over and swamp us for a while.

A lot later we may even learn to welcome
the occasional rogue wave of sadness
a memento of someone we loved
and of how much we loved them.

Foreword

If death takes someone we love then we have to struggle with our grief. If it happens when we are a child then we have fewer resources and less experience to fall back on. It can be very hard.

This book contains four stories woven together:

- a description of the journey by bike across northern England that I made to visit places connected with my childhood: a journey ending in Withernsea
- the story of how my parents came to meet in Withernsea in 1949 and what happened to our family around the time of my father's accident and subsequent death
- how as a nine year old child I dealt with his loss
- the therapeutic journey I made as an adult to try to uncover the nature of my grief and, more importantly, to try to transcend and transform it

I hope that you will join me on these journeys.

Home

I come awake, and it's still dark. Outside, I can hear the wind gusting and blustering to gale force. I hear the wind thrashing in the trees and the rain driving down. This is the morning of my leaving, and soon I will have to cast myself out into the grey dawn and the elemental forces that will meet me and beat me.

Leaving the home that I know, leaving the safety and warmth with which I am familiar, to enter what I can now hear and imagine, seems a nonsensical thing to do. Inwardly, I feel my reluctance transform into anxiety and then fear. I lie rigidly for a while in my bed, listening to the forces outside, and wrestling with the forces inside.

I have been planning this journey for a long time. I have been looking forward to this morning of departure for a long time also. I have chosen to travel in autumn because it feels the right time of year for the journey. I had hoped for an Indian summer, with soft light and the muted autumnal colours of decay. But instead I have gales. This is the equinox, so I have equinoctial gales.

There is no escape. I have too much invested to back out now. Reluctantly I face what I have to do. I know the score in these situations. I have to take one step at a time till the next step is due. My fear is only fear. Fear too will pass, and movement will help it pass, help it transform into a different energy. That's the theory. But those forces out there are powerful, and in here I'm a tight knot of reluctance.

I get myself upright and out of bed. I draw the curtains and make myself look into the reality of the world out there. Just how bad is it? I have to know.

There is no point in not knowing any longer. Where is the wind coming from? This is the crucial factor.

There is enough light to see the upper branches of the trees across the way bending and jostling each other as they succumb to the forces of the gale. I see that the wind is from the west. It will be behind me. It is good news. It makes my journey possible.

I open the window and try to sense the quality of the rain. It is being driven by the wind and coming down hard, diagonally, in squally bursts. The ground is very wet, with large puddles formed on the track.

As I look out at what I am being given, I feel another sense of relief. I realise I can also manage the rain, because the wind will be behind me. I have new waterproofs. There's a good chance I will stay reasonably dry. My feet will get wet fast, but there is no helping that. My trip is still on, and I need to leave soon, in the dawn, to maximise my chances of reaching my first night's lodging before night falls. There is only a certain amount of daylight and I have a long way to go. It is equinox: equal day, and equal night; everything, for the moment, in balance.

There is little for me to do before leaving, because I have prepared everything carefully the night before. The usual ablutions; a little breakfast, which, disliking bright electric light in the mornings, I eat in twilight in the kitchen.

In the small stone-built lobby of our old stone-built farmhouse home, my bike awaits me, panniers packed. I am surrounded by what is familiar: the coats on the pegs, the shoes on the racks, the onions harvested from the garden waiting to be strung up. At the moment of leaving they assume a comforting force, a pull to remain. In here it all feels cosy and safe; out there it sounds wild and not safe.

I put on hat, waterproof jacket, and waterproof trousers. I put on a fluorescent belt in order to attempt to advertise my presence to inattentive car drivers. I switch on my bike lights and unbolt the door. I hear a noise in the house, and wonder if it's the cats, or whether Mary is coming down to bid me farewell. It's another reason to linger for another minute or two.

Mary appears. She has come downstairs to bid me farewell. She hugs me, and wishes me a good journey. I open our heavy old oak door, with the decayed bits on the bottom that I have tried to patch up over the years. Maybe I could just stay here and work on that for the next few days? Too late, mate, out you go! It is 6.40am.

Out

Outside, I am momentarily sheltered by the gable end of the house from the full force of the wind and rain, but as I push the bike, with its unfamiliar high handlebars, and unfamiliar heavy load, up the path and through the gate, I come out from the lee of the house and into the full force of the weather. I bend my head down to avoid the worst of the driving rain. The rain increases as I pause to gather myself together in these testing surroundings. The sound of the rain on my jacket, and on the ground, confirms I have decided to leave at the moment when the rain has decided to renew its onslaught. I push off along the track and pedal. I am moving, despite the rain.

I experience again that peculiar sense of satisfaction and pleasure which comes from moving forward on so unlikely a vehicle as a bicycle. The miracle of balancing on two wheels, of moving forward faster than walking but with less effort, works its magic. I briefly remember my friend David Hogg, and learning to ride his bike one sunny afternoon when I was five. Then I am back to the present reality of a gloomy early autumnal morning in driving rain. I successfully manoeuvre the first steep bend on the track, and then the drain running right across the track. I manage the very steep short hill down, and the tight bend at the bottom. Plenty of caution and plenty of brake power. It would not do to crash or fall off at this very early stage. Too embarrassing by far.

A short uphill takes me to the junction with the road. The rain is more visible in the beam of my front light than in the twilight that surrounds me. The road is quiet and traffic free. It is very early. Sensible folk are still at home, in bed.

I turn on to the road and head east, the wind powerfully behind me. It strikes me that I am actually on my journey, that I have started. I want to think about my plans, and what I hope to achieve, and be aware of the whole process, but the survival needs are too strong. The practicalities are, at this moment, the whole process. There is no space for anything else.

I must get up the hill that faces me. To do that I have to concentrate on the gears of the bike, which are still so new to me that I have to think about them – which lever do I push to change them in the right direction? I keep glancing down at the front chainwheel and rear sprockets to check that the chain is running in the kind of place I expect it to run to get me up the hill. I also need to listen out for any unfamiliar noises that might presage disaster. My drive mechanism is being subjected to large forces: I am carrying a fair amount of stuff, and I am going uphill. Yesterday evening I had to take the wheels off several times – did I put them back on correctly? If anything goes wrong now, then serious damage could result. Crunching and grinding noises accompanied by that sick feeling in the guts.

I must deal with the potential threat of traffic. I must listen out for engine noises behind me so that I can be on my guard if a vehicle passes me. Some of them have a habit of cutting in too finely. I need to be alert, and be aware of the wind's force, and avoid suddenly being blown further out into the roadway.

I have to deal with the rain, and the experience of cycling while water cascades down on to me, and splashes back up on to me from the road, and gets on to my glasses and obscures my view, even though I am wearing a hat with a brim, held on by my hood.

And I have to get up this hill, through my own energetic efforts, through the force of my own muscles and willpower. I have driven this hill hundreds of times. I have applied a relaxed right foot to the accelerator pedal of my car and sped up whilst getting myself more comfortable in the seat and thinking about whether I can do the next fifty miles in under an hour. Now I push the gear lever on my handlebar so that the really huge sprocket is brought into action. I am in my lowest gear, pedalling fast in order to travel at slow walking pace. I keep my legs turning. There is effort involved, but it is not a draining effort. It is sustainable, and I sustain it until I reach the top of the bank, where the gradient eases off as the hill continues to climb more gently. The wind, at the moment, is my friend, and pushes me from behind.

At the very top of the hill there is a mobile phone mast set off to the left. A few yards along the track to it there is a place where I think I can shelter a little from the rain and wind. I want to catch my breath and adjust my hood. It's a little too tight so it pulls the brim of my hat too far down. I can comfortably see the ground, but if I want to look ahead, I have to tip my head back, which puts a strain on my neck. On a bike, when my physical energy is the only fuel I have, then it's important to conserve it as much as possible, and use it up as conservatively as possible. If I'm to make it to the end of a long journey, then I have to pay attention to the detail of my body. One awkward twist of my neck may be manageable, but lots of awkward twists over a long period will cause big problems.

I turn left on to the little track which has several big puddles on it, and as I ride through the first one, my foot goes down into the water and gets its first proper soaking. I feel the cold water squelching round my toes.

The wall is a disappointment as far as shelter is concerned. The wind is so strong that I do not notice any lessening effect at all. I hurriedly make adjustments to my hood, and leave again, so I can get the wind behind me. I recycle through the puddle, but avoid the deepest parts. I am back on the road, but the hood adjustment, like many things done in a hurry, is only partially successful. It will have to be readjusted at the next stop. For the moment, my desire is just to keep moving, to maintain my momentum on this journey. The further I get from home, the harder it will be to succumb to any temptation to turn round and head back there.

I progress at speed now through the wet and the rain, for my trend is downhill, and the strong winds behind me push me forcefully along. On my right the valley of the River Wenning, and Burn Moor beyond, are hidden in the gloom and the rain and the cloud. On my left the familiar flat-topped presence of Ingleborough is likewise obscured.

Ingleborough's striking profile, unmistakably visible for miles around, has been a feature of my home territory for the nearly twenty years I have lived here. The remains of a large, wide, stone-built wall round the top were thought to be ramparts, evidence of a defensive Iron Age position. Circular outlines still visible on the flat and exposed summit plateau were thought to be the remnants of hut circles. There is a theory that the Romans attacked and defeated an Iron Age tribe holed up here. I've always felt that the Iron Age fort theory didn't stack up – even in summer the weather and exposure at over 2000 feet can be deadly, never mind the labour of hauling supplies up, or the problem of a reliable water source. So I was gratified to hear a local archaeologist recently tell us that there was no evidence for the Roman theory, no dating evidence for the Iron Age theory, and that the ramparts were of a type unknown from any other Iron Age site. Instead, a more recent theory suggests a Bronze Age date for the remains, and that Ingleborough was used as a sacred mountain particularly associated with ceremonies for those who have died.

That immediately felt right to me. Ever since, whenever I have seen it, instead of thinking 'last hiding place of free Britons about to be killed or enslaved by the Roman machine' I have thought 'extraordinary natural feature utilised by ancient peoples to mark and announce their wonder and respect for the processes of life and death.' Today, actually, I cannot see it at all, but even though it is invisible, its presence is with me.

My own journey is about death. It is a pilgrimage into my past. From it I hope to find out more about my present, and gain guidance for my future. I am bereft of the close tribal community that would have surrounded me here in the Bronze Age. It would have mediated my relations with the forces beyond life, and provided structure and support in the face of death. Instead, cut loose also from the strictures of a traditional society, I am free to make my solitary way across the territory of my life, and draw from it such meaning and conclusions as twenty-first century western thought will allow me.

A change to the landscape through which I am moving is upon me. Enclosed green pastures are about to give way to a stretch of rough, open moorland. A farm marks the threshold, and the trees that surround it promise a whisper of shelter. I pause on a cropped verge, and prop my bike against a convenient stone wall that has caught my eye. A few yards away, half a dozen wet sheep, apparently also sheltering, gaze at me with mild interest, and I gaze back. We are all wrong about the shelter, for it does not exist, and the wind blows, and the rain streams, with undiluted force. There is nothing to be gained from pausing here. There is only body heat to be lost. Only movement onward has validity and sense. There is no choice; I remount the bike, and conscious of the cold and wet feet that propel me, give the sheep a wide berth and head on down the road.

Moor

The moor is a boggy landscape which today fits particularly well with the elemental force of the weather. The sound of the wind and the driving rain splattering on to my waterproofs dominates my hearing. The solitary nature of my existence within encircling walls of gloom and rain and mist is broken only occasionally by the headlights of cars, the rain glinting profusely in the light of their beams.

The road swoops up and down. Therefore my work is easy – to keep pedalling, and use only two gears, a big one for going downhill, and then a little one when the road swoops up again.

This is my home territory. I have driven this road hundreds of times, collecting children after school, going shopping, racing to meet people off trains – all the small change and common currency of family life. I have never, however, experienced it like this, and in the rain, and cold, and wind, and effort, I am exhilarated by the experience. What had inevitably tended towards becoming commonplace and routine is now new and fresh.

As I feel my knees and thighs rise and fall rhythmically, and hear the splishing of the fat tyres on the wet road, I feel a surge of excitement rise in me at the journey ahead. If the first few miles can give me such intensity, what might the rest of the trip not produce?

My aim is to make a journey across northern England. Day by day, I will be progressing eastwards into the future, into the unknown. I hope to be open enough to the unknown for it to remain with me, a companion on my journey. The unknown is always interesting, and always challenging, but it does not deal solely in pleasure.

In addition, I will be making a journey into my past. By heading in a rough line towards the coast, my itinerary will neatly take in several physical locations that have been important to my emotional journey, to my inner development. In particular, at this autumn season, I want to revisit the territories connected with my father, who died when I was nine.

These territories are not alien to me. Over the years, I have revisited many times the emotional landscape - of anger and misery and sorrow and love – connected with those times. I have been searching, as is usual in circumstances of loss, for relief from grief, for understanding, for peace and tranquility, for the capacity and strength to continue to live, and love. I have often found what I needed, and found ways to channel my searching energies creatively, but the quest to find out more remains. A searching self is never satisfied – there is always the next crest.

So, on this journey, I intend to visit places I know well, visit places I have not returned to since childhood, and visit places to which I have never been but which are yet important to my history. From the physical connections I hope to glean clues to the truth of what happened then, and what has happened since. I want to go on and add these gleanings to the granary of my personal history, and from the store of old and new mixed together, create a freshly kneaded and proved and baked version of the truth. This might then be shared in good company, and, who knows, provide fresh sustenance for all.

Crossroads

The road dips down. The slope and the powerful driving wind from right behind me make progress effortless. Circumstances, however, as ever, are about to change. Ahead of me is a crossroads, and my route, designed to keep me on minor roads away from traffic, requires that I turn right. The prospects seem uncertain, and the reality turns out, in fact, to be painful. As I turn right on to the small road which undulates across boggy, unfenced common land, the wind drives the rain into the unprotected right side of my face, a continual stinging assault, the pain of which forces me to turn my face away. Steering at once becomes hazardous, a matter of a steady focus on the left hand verge of the road a few yards in front interspersed with quick glances ahead out of the corner of my eye. The wind is also turned from a back pusher to a side shover, and I have to concentrate carefully to deal with the strongest gusts which try their best to deposit me in the boggy badlands alongside the road.

I pass the place where, in summer, travellers on their way to and from the horse fair at Appleby still park their caravans together and camp, sitting companionably round a campfire while suspicious locals in their cars pass within a few feet. I see the indistinct remains of the railway branch line that was Beechinged in the sixties, but which must have been a travel lifeline to several generations of local people, suspicious or not. And with the rain having been falling for hours, I see a moor sodden and saturated, with water pooling and seeping and running in all the places to be expected, and more beside.

In two or three places, small streamlets in ditches have expanded to flood their way across the road, and I re-experience the joy, first encountered in childhood, of riding a bike through standing water; of seeing the water part beneath the leading tyre like the waters of the Red Sea, of seeing it splash up and out and around, and of hearing the splooshh sound that accompanies it. I raise my feet off the pedals in time honoured fashion, to minimise their chances of getting wet, but as they are already wet through the purpose is in the sensation, not in the usefulness.

After a while, the road trends more south east than south, and I gain corresponding relief from the wind and rain. In addition, a high stone wall and a hillside on my right provide further protection. Relief comes in other forms too, as daylight has increased to the point now where I realise I can safely turn my bike lights off. And with daylight has come a change in the weather. The wind is blowing as fiercely as ever, but the clouds have lifted and broken up, and the rain is ceasing. I look for a suitable place to stop, rest, and make adjustments.

Gateway

A recessed gateway in the stone wall on my right provides the necessary resources for a halt: something to lean the bike against, a good place to stand safely off the road, and some shelter from the wind. I get off and wander around a little, checking out my body to see whether the unaccustomed exertions have done any lasting damage. As yet, as far as I can tell, all remains relatively well, and for that I am suitably grateful. My anxieties focus particularly around the comfort of the saddle and the pain potentially caused to the relevant area of my body by a prolonged ride when I am so out of practice. In the several years since I have stopped riding a bike with anything like regularity (pressures of work, pressures of taxiing children in a rural area etc etc) - in those years I have grown a little thinner and bonier with age as some of my muscle bulk has dropped away. The odd recent ride on my old bike with its unforgiving Brookes leather saddle has produced impressive aches and pain in a short time. (The unforgiving drop handlebars didn't do my back any favours either.)

So when I bought my new bike for this trip, I was keen to get a broad, soft, comfy saddle. (And also genteel sit-up-and-beg handlebars.) Not only did I get a comfy saddle, but I also discovered that since the last time I went anywhere near a new bike (admittedly a couple of decades ago) technology had wrought such wonders as a sprung seat stem to act as a shock absorber, and a saddle that moves slightly from side to side with the pedalling motion in order, I presume, to minimise friction and soreness in those important nether regions. I was now the proud owner of said technology, and, so far, it was working well. No pain in the arse for me.

Looking around, I see that although the rain has now ceased, and daylight has arrived, conditions are still dramatic. Brooding dark grey clouds race by close overhead. My route here is skirting the flanks of Burn Moor, and, in the mid distance, only its lowest slopes are visible, while cloud cover swathes all else. Right next to me, some young whippy birch trees thrash and jump around in the wind, the notes of the wind in the leaves varying with the movement of the branches as well as the change in velocity of the gusts.

I turn off my bike lights, take them off their brackets, and put them away in the pannier pocket. I undo the drawstrings of my hood, and pull it down. It is a relief to let a little more air into my life and escape the mild claustrophobia that a tightly tied hood produces for me. I am still well protected from the elements, as my peaked cap has ear flaps which come right down to fasten under my chin with Velcro. This is a somewhat ridiculous looking piece of headgear, which I normally only wear very early in the morning when wandering over the fields near my home, as I am too embarrassed to be seen wearing it in public. However, on a day like today, its capacity to remain on my head in the wind outweighs my embarrassment (just) and it stays on.

My feet squelch horribly and coldly when I walk, but the rest of me seems to be completely dry. I am surprised. I know my jacket and overtrousers are new, and that they are meant to keep me dry, but I think I am so used to my familiar old gear, which stopped being more than tokenly waterproof some considerable time ago, that I find the lack of damp completely unexpected.

There is nowhere to sit, and no reason to linger, and every reason to move on, so, mounting my bike again, that is what I do.   .

Waves

Past the pub where I picked up my son and other drunken teenagers after the school karaoke night. Past the house where Mary bought a car from a man who had commuted to Blackpool in it. Past (the other) Clapham station, a little halt looking down over the river. Under the railway, then past another house where someone used to live who I used to know, who had hit someone in the pub for having an affair with his wife. Over the river, swollen and frothing and racing past beneath. Turn left along a road that Mary and I walked along when the foot and mouth restrictions stopped us walking on the footpaths for so long. These are reminders that this is still my home territory, over which I have roamed while my children grew up, and which is marked at every turn by memory and experience.

I come to a hill, a steep bank, and I decide to adopt the hill climbing tactics which I used to use on long bike journeys when I last did them (before children). This involves getting off and walking. Pretty well every time. The advantages of this approach are: I use a different set of muscles and rest my cycling ones, I get to look at the scenery instead of fighting the pedals, I get to avoid exhausting myself, I get to feel humble and slightly pathetic (though also, strangely, I get to feel superior to those whose pride won't let them get off and walk), and

I get to practice slowing down and taking the long view on matters.

So here I am walking up this steep little bank, pushing my bike, and one of my rewards for this sacrificial act of humility is that I notice the water flowing down the road. It is not a stream, but a widespread shallow front, on whose surface a regular pattern of tiny waves progresses with regal stateliness. Green and yellowing birch leaves, torn from their branches by the autumn gales, lie scattered about on the tarmac, as though waiting for the wavelets to move over and carry them away to pastures new.

My other reward is to encounter two tups from the adjoining field, who come crowding up to a gateway to watch me as I approach. I pause to admire them, and contemplate the diet of sexual feast and famine that is their lot. My own lot at this moment is to keep pushing my bike up hill, which is what I proceed to do.

Comfort

From the top of the bank I have a descent along a ridge, and then I'm back under the railway again. The road crosses over a small stream, which is surging along its course with visible power, tugging at the grass and bushes along its banks.

The road goes up and down, and consequently I get off and push, and get on and freewheel. I cross and recross the railway. I go through a hamlet with its brand new village hall. The weather brightens even more. There is a hint of sunshine behind the lowering clouds. The green of the countryside is strong and vibrant even in the dull conditions.

After a while I realise that I have cycled this little section previously. A few years before I had come out on a Sunday morning with my bike on the back of the car, parked nearby, and cycled around for a few hours. I had come out to escape a bout of desperation and misery and loneliness and depression, but of course the feelings were mine and came with me. Now the landscape around me is being re-coloured with paler versions of the feelings from that time. Back then I had sought to attach the misery to causes that I could blame and thus remove the misery from me to them. When we suffer we usually take whatever measures we can to alleviate it. My targets were the normal ones in these circumstances: those closest to me – family life, the children, Mary. Now I wonder whether that attack of misery and depression, and others like it over the years, did not have an earlier root. How did I manage, aged nine, in those months and years after my father died? What was going on back then?

His death happened during the Christmas holidays, so that when I went back to school for the new term, my mother gave me a note for Miss Rhind, my elderly spinster class teacher. My mother explained that it was important the school knew. There was an implication I picked up that if I got upset then the school needed to be aware of why it might be so. I took the letter to Miss Rhind at her desk in the terrapin building attached to the school which was our classroom for that year. I watched her closely as she opened the note. She was about to find out what I myself had found out only a week or so before. How do people react to the news of death? How would she deal with this small boy in front of her who has just lost his father? She read the note, glanced at me, and looked away. She hurriedly put the letter back in the envelope, put it away, and then thanked me in a way I understood as a dismissal. I went back to the table I shared with some other children.

Mrs Peel, on the other hand showed a lot of upset when she found out. She was our neighbour, a very domestic woman with two daughters, one of whom was a lot older than me, and one younger. It was in the very early days after we got the news. Things were strange, not normal. Hearing a noise on our driveway, I came out of the house to see Mrs Peel approaching my mother, her face twisted with grief, sobbing, tears. 'I've just heard, I've just heard,' she was saying, though the words were hard to distinguish amidst her loss of control. She was reaching out to my mother, and my mother, there on the driveway, took her in hand and comforted her. I remember thinking how strange it was that my mother, at this very difficult time for her, should be the one to offer comfort.

As I remember these incidents, I can also feel my reluctance to do so. Those were painful times, and the pain, though diminished, lingers on in association with the memories. It is probably the pain, the emotional intensity, I realise, that keeps the memories so clear. And yet here I am heading off on a journey that will deliberately put me in positions where these memories will be restimulated. No wonder I feel a little anxiety, a little fear about this journey.

Hunger

As I cycle, content to make steady if unspectacular progress, a chorus from a song comes into my mind and spins around in it, refusing to either leave or resolve into the whole song, which would at least provide me with entertainment. It is a Leonard Cohen chorus, from his recent album. I hear my internal voice singing in a Leonard-style deep gravelly bass, or as close to it as my normally tenor inclined internal voice can get: 'And when the hunger for your touch, rises from the hunger...' The phrase goes round and round, and on and on, as these things can do, until I am forced to look at it more carefully. I love many Leonard Cohen songs for the sense they give me of a tenuous and ungraspable connection with things beyond my normal reach. Often when I listen more carefully to the words I get a series of images that on their own don't make much sense to me and don't seem to connect with each other either. And yet... there is something being communicated, creating tantalising hints of another reality.

I realise I don't know which song this line is from, or even whether I have the words right. I am only confident about the tune. But in my brain at this moment, the meaning is clear. The hunger is the longing that Rumi, and the Sufis, talk about. The longing for God, for union, for The One, for enlightenment, a longing whose force can be described in language that is normally used to describe sexual passion and the desire drive. And the connection is not just linguistic, for the implication is that the energy that drives towards spiritual connection is also the energy of sexual connection, but an energy that has been transcended (gone beyond, but still included, though transformed, not suppressed or denied). And a further implication is clear too – that love is the key, in both areas, to maintaining and developing the connection. Is that what I have to do, I wonder, and if so, how can I do it, weak as I am?

'And when the hunger for your touch, rises from the hunger...'

I come to a minor crossroads close to the Settle bypass, and pause. I think my route will take me to the right, but I want to check the map and look around. Two small buses pass me. They are Bibby buses, the local coach firm, and they are taking children to school. One or other of my children has caught Bibby buses to this school for the last six years, but no more. My daughter's friends may still be on one of those buses, but, she, my youngest, has now left home. I am in the new and unknown emotional territory of childlessness.

The buses remind me I am still on physical home territory, but only just. I am now edging into territory I know I have never cycled before.

A Townson's fuel lorry passes me and a pungent smell of fuel oil, bitter and unpleasant, permeates the air. I will have to follow it up the road, which is bad enough, but worse, the lorry has stopped and is waiting a short way down the road, while a herd of cattle is marshalled across the road. Lowing cattle and throbbing lorry engine fill the air with their different sounds and different smells.

I am anxious to get going now because the wind is still blowing hard, and I have cooled down and am feeling chilly. I am uncomfortably aware of my wet feet, and also that I am not wearing a jumper under my fleece and jacket. Temperature control is harder to manage under these more variable conditions. In the meantime the sun has developed from a hint behind the clouds to a full grown presence, and for that at least I am grateful. As it is still early in the morning, the light cast by the sun is low, and, as I finally set off again, the details of the humps and dips of the land are picked out in exquisite relief.

Synchronous

The pleasure of the freewheel is intense. I am sweeping down an incline towards the railway again, gathering yet more free speed. It is not really free, for I paid for it with a push up a hill, but that was at least several minutes ago, and I have forgotten that now. As I turn a bend, the low morning sun shines on the wet road so powerfully and so wonderfully, that I am blinded by the reflected light, and forced to put on the brakes and ride more temperately. As I arrive at a short tunnel under the railway and pause in the relative shelter afforded, I find myself smiling at the experience, and, as is often the case, rather wishing I had a convivial companion to share it with. I think of my oldest son Ewan, with whom I have shared several pleasurable rides – he would have enjoyed the swoop, and the sunlight, and the speed, and we would have shared in the pleasure, and laughed at each other afterwards.

I remember that he is going through a slightly difficult patch at the moment, and remind myself to phone or text him later. A car passes me, and I notice that the letters of its number plate are the same as his initials. Hmmm...synchronous. More pleasure, more smiling, but still alone.

Because my father died when I was nine, I have no experience of a father's relationship with his adult sons. In fact, as soon as my oldest got to be ten, I was in unknown territory. While having no closely felt model to follow was difficult, the advantage was that I was not hamstrung by too powerful or familiar a structure. I was free to make it up as I went along, and to pick and choose what I liked from other fathers, and other sources.

In fact my primary aim as a father was to stay alive as long as possible. When Ewan got to be ten, I quietly celebrated the fact that I'd survived longer than my father, and that my sons would be able to remember more of me than my brother and I could of our father. And now I had succeeded in going on and even further on, so that I was father to two young men leading (relatively) independent lives. How strange that I should have two adults as my sons, when, inside, a large chunk of me still feels stuck at the age of nine. And how strange too that their grandfather, whom they have never known, should remain stuck, for me, at age thirty-nine, the age he died, and a lot younger than I am now. In this confusing scenario, I am the oldest; my father is younger than I am, but older than his grandsons; and they in their turn are older than me their father, who is also the youngest as well as the oldest.

Emerging from the tunnel, I have to manage a short section along the Settle bypass before being able to turn off the main road again and head for the byways. The traffic is fierce enough to scare a cyclist fresh from the hills, and the few hundred yards before my right turn are quite long enough.

As a vehicle on the road, it is of course my entitlement to signal right, pull over to the right hand side of my carriageway, and wait in the middle until a suitable gap in the oncoming traffic affords me an opportunity to turn into my side road. Given that on this long straight modern road (I watched them build it from the trains I commuted on when the children were little), the traffic is toying with, or possibly even exceeding the sixty speed limit, I decline the opportunity and wait on the left hand side of my carriageway. Then, feeling like a rabbit out of Watership Down, I scuttle across the whole road in relative safety, and scoot off on my lesser road to Rathmell, a tiny village a couple of miles further on.

Except, when I get on it, my lesser road has its own version of a rush hour – the Rathmell rush hour - and streams of cars shoot past me in both directions. Where are they going? Where am I going? What is this frantic madness we are all caught up in?

I am now approaching the river Ribble, into whose territory I am headed. The Ribble, as it often does, has taken notice of the prolific rainfall by flooding the fields alongside. If I did not know there was a river there, I would assume it was a lake. At one point the water lies right up against the stone wall that divides the road from the fields. A couple of trees emerge strangely from the middle of the water. Cows graze unconcernedly in their changed surroundings. The light from a watery sun reflects off the surface of the water.

Further down the road I see where the water has seeped through the wall and flooded a length of road of about fifty yards. I watch as various cars create a performance at this point. Some wait and gather up their courage before entering, and creep along down the centre of the road where it might be shallowest. Others, from foreknowledge or foolhardiness, plunge straight in and plough through at the best speed they can make, sending water cascading all around.

When it is my turn, I wait until the road is clear (don't want to be soaked by one of the plunging types), and then cycle through. I enjoy the experience very much. The water level (in the middle of the road) is just below the level of my pedals, and my feet, wet though they are, are spared a further soaking.

Rathmell has sensibly set itself on the escarpment above the floodplain, so in order to get up there I have to get off and walk, and push. My feet squelch wetly and coldly. I badly want them to be drier and warmer again. Survival, and practical matters, urge themselves into my consciousness, and won't be denied. I finally admit to myself that I have some better socks in my bag. These will keep my feet warmer, even when wet, and it would really be sensible to change into them. I have actually known this for some time, but the practicalities involved - stopping, searching, removing, drying, replacing etc – were so onerous, that I preferred to remain in denial mode. Ah well, better give in to sensibleness. Perhaps Rathmell will have a bench to offer, where the deed may be done.

Rathmell

Under increasingly darkening skies, I hit Rathmell. A road junction, a few stone-built houses, some large trees and a church. As the rain starts to fall again, I swing my bike round towards the reading room, situated opposite the church, and by the road junction. The reading room has a porch, also stone built, but open at the front, and generously enough proportioned that I can get my bike in at one side and me in at the other. Old men from times past have kindly provided me with a bench to sit on, and I gratefully sit on it. Those old men must have sat here too in times past, sheltering from the rain, or from the sun. Outside, now, the rain comes down with renewed vigour, and the wind flings the rain about in gusty squalls. From the comparative shelter of my viewpoint, it's enjoyable.

Rathmell may be tiny, and it may be raining, but it is not quiet. A steady stream of cars passes me, and, as many of them are turning left at the junction, they slow down right by me. I cannot help noticing them, and they, presumably, cannot help noticing me. I feel more exposed to public view than I am strictly comfortable with, but as the elements seem to intend me to remain here for a while, then I retreat from discomfort behind one of my habitual defences. In this case it is an inflated sense of kinship with the important: 'I may look like a waif and stray who can't afford a proper car, but actually I'm on a journey of self-discovery. You're just driving a big 4x4 with a personalized number plate.' I remember years before, sitting in an employment office in Sheffield and watching an old dosser going round carefully collecting discarded cigarette butts. After a while, aware that various people were watching him, some perhaps with mild criticism in their hearts, he looked up and addressed the room at large in his broad Glaswegian accent; 'The queen, y'know, in Buck'nam Palace, she does this.'

As well as cars, there are real people wandering by. A man goes to the church, and waves to another man. A woman hurries past, well wrapped up against the weather.

I decide that postponement can be justified no longer, and rummage through my panniers and find the better socks in question. I also find my towel – one of those scraps of cloth like a dish cloth that's meant to be super absorbent and save weight. I remain unconvinced as to whether they actually work. I set to work anyway, removing socks and shoes, emptying surplus water from shoes, drying feet, putting on warm socks, sighing with pleasure, putting wet shoes back on, not sighing with pleasure. I do all this while cars pass and pause nearby, and I feel somewhat vulnerable. Only my feet are bare, but I feel a little as though I'm in one of those dreams where you suddenly find yourself naked in public. Or have I dreamt that other people have those dreams too? Is it actually only me that has that dream?

I feel the hint of a longing for my dad to be there to protect and guide me at times of vulnerability. As a boy I had to make my own way, and protect myself, and understand how to do it. We all have to do that, but I had to do that more on my own than I wanted. A good dad can ease your way into the difficult outside world. That's what I assume they can do, and what I've seen friends do with their sons, and what I've tried to do with mine. At the time I was growing up, I didn't know that that was what was missing. I knew I felt alone and vulnerable at times. I knew I just missed my dad.

I have something to eat, and something to drink, and check out the map. If I were to go down the side road at this junction, I could come to a farm called Black Leach, another called Sheep Wash, and one called Rome. There is also a place called Wham. Sadly, I must leave these exotica for another time. Today, I am called instead to Wigglesworth.

Trapeze

The rain, which had eased off while I was in the porch, decides to increase almost as soon as I am on the road again. I cycle on, my feet now in relative comfort, as the rain pours down around me. My waterproofs continue to do their job, and there is a pleasure in cheating the elements in this way. As if responding to the challenge implicit in this rash thought, the rain intensifies, until I am cycling in the Yorkshire equivalent of a tropical downpour. Rain is drilling down and splattering and bouncing on the road until I am cycling through a thick layer of spray several inches high. The noise, particularly where the rain is hitting my hood and shoulders, is impressive. I pass a barn, and am tempted to shelter, but there is no obvious way in, the roof looks a bit dodgy, and then, anyway, I am past, and to turn back would be to turn into the driving wind and torrential rain. Instead I keep my head down and keep going.

After a while I agree to be more respectful in future, and the rain agrees to ease off. The Ribble valley is visible below on my left, with flooded fields accompanying the river's meandering procession like beads on a necklace. I pass a cattery, and the barn where a group of us had, only a couple of months before, performed a play about the whole of life taking place on a tram. The tram made its rattling, prescribed journey and at every stop, people got on, and people got off. We had a rowing couple and a courting couple, we had performers and music, eccentrics and strays. Life on the tram had included sex, an orgasm, birth and a death. We had had a real coffin on stage, brought on by two undertakers.

When my father died, there was a funeral, but my brother and I did not go to it. In those days, it was not considered advisable for children to be exposed to the distressing realities of the ceremonies associated with death. This was, I have no doubt, a well-meant attempt to protect and look after us. It would have fitted with the general taboo around death that persists in our culture, though now somewhat diminished, up to the present day.

One of the consequences of this was that I never got the chance to say goodbye. I had said goodbye to him a few days before he died, when he headed off to hospital for a few days for a check-up. He did this periodically, and I had expected to see him again shortly. He never returned, and I never saw him again.

He was going for a hospital check-up because he had had an accident, three years previously in October

1958. He was a physical training instructor in the Navy, based at the PT school in Portsmouth. He was demonstrating an exercise on a trapeze over the swimming baths, which involved diving into the pool at the end. He hit his head on the bottom, broke his neck, and was left paralysed. Unable to move, he held his breath and waited for help. The men on the side thought he was fooling around, as men do, until they noticed blood in the water, then they dived in and dragged him out.

I come to Wigglesworth and take a left turn. The rain has stopped, but the wind still blows fiercely. My route takes me downhill towards the river and a crossing at Cow Bridge.

The accident brought our normal family existence to an abrupt end. I have some memories of that period before the accident – of visits by relatives, of starting school, of playing with friends – and they are the usual memories of a child growing up in a loving family environment. But one day he must have gone off to work, and never come back, and after that, for a period, my memories are sparse.

But there are other sources to help me grasp what happened. My mother has told me how she found out. A man from the PT school came to the door on his way home. We lived in married quarters, and he probably lived nearby. He said that there had been an accident at work and Ernie, my dad, had been taken to hospital. He didn't say how bad it was. Perhaps he didn't know, or maybe he did know but didn't want to say. My mother says she knew immediately that something was badly wrong, left us boys with the neighbour, and rushed to the phone box at the end of the street.

'I was so anxious, my hands were shaking so much, I couldn't get my money in. I had to make myself calm down, so that I could speak to the hospital.' After making contact, she went straight to the hospital. They told her how bad it was, that he was paralysed from the neck down, and that he would never recover. They also said it was better if he was not told, but realised it himself, gradually, over a period of time. She spent the next period listening to him making plans for what they would do after he got better.

A little later, the doctors decided he would be better off at Stoke Mandeville, a hospital near Aylesbury specialising in spinal injuries. He was flown there direct by helicopter, with some medical staff and my mother also as passengers. There had never been a direct flight there before, and my mother has told me they put out white sheets on the ground to mark the landing space.

I have seen glossy black and white press photos of the event, with my mother standing at the edge looking on. My dad, on a trolley, is being dealt with by doctors, and orderlies, and nurses with their quaint old-fashioned nurses' hats. The helicopter is there as the backdrop.

Other photos come to mind, that tell some of the subsequent story.

A glossy picture of my dad in an iron lung, a large metal box covering his entire chest area and just his head poking out the top. This was so he could breathe, I was told, as his own lungs weren't working. He was essentially being kept alive in a big metal box.

A photo of him with weights attached to his head and led over a pulley, in order to keep his neck stretched, looking a little like a medieval torture. Do I really remember that, or is it some kind of awfulness that my memory has created? I'm not sure.

A photo of the ward: a big room, spacious, light, airy, opening on to the grounds outside. Full of beds down both sides. Some men sitting up, some in wheel chairs, some lying turned to face the camera, some flat on their backs.

Photos

Cow Bridge is long and low, with plenty of room for the floodwaters to pass under. Just across the other side, I take a right turn up a minor road that feels like it sees little traffic, which is just the way I like my roads. Past a few contractors working on a building, I pause by a gateway. Gnarled grown-out hawthorn bushes line small embankments on both sides of the road. The fields round here look underused and forgotten.

In the distance Pendle Hill rears its distinctive bulk up into the air. George Fox had a mystical vision from the top, and from that vision followed, after much suffering, the growth of the Quakers. Find that of God within. Rely not upon the priests to mediate with the Lord. The body of the church is the people who worship, not the buildings made with hands. Swear not oaths, for there should only be truth. Use not violence against others but treat all with love and tenderness. We are all equal before the Lord God.

Inside me is a picture of my dad that comes mostly from photographs, because my actual memories are so few and uncertain at this age. There are many photos: small, square, black and white. My dad in shorts and singlet in the hot sun of Malta with me on his knee. My dad on the beach with my brother and I. My dad, wearing fifties style wide trousers and a jacket, on a park bench with my brother and I. My dad lying on the floor at a kids party, smiling, while many small children sit on top of him.

The many photos live in boxes, and I have revisited them through the years. My few memories live inside me, and I likewise revisit them through the years. Here's one: I have a stick, and I want the bark peeled off. I go to my dad to ask him to do it for me, with his penknife. He smiles at me and asks would I like it doing in a checkerboard pattern, and he demonstrates a little to show me. I look and say, no, what I really want is for all the bark to come off, and he smiles again and does it for me.

It's time to get moving again. I have a slight uphill to negotiate, but it's within my capacity, and I pedal up and over a slight rise, and then down to a junction with a main road. There's no avoiding the next mile of cycling on a busy road, and I'm not looking forward to it. At the junction, there are a couple of old stone houses, built very close to the road. I wait until some seriously sized lorries have gone past, then launch myself into the madness that is vehicular traffic.

If I pedal madly then it will all be over quicker. I have to look out for a left turn into a small lane about a mile ahead. I'm looking out now, though I've only travelled a hundred and fifty yards. No sign yet. Cars whizz past me on both sides of the road. They all miss me.

I am so busy surviving the dangers, real and imagined, of the road, that when the side road comes I almost miss it. Concentrating on pedalling up a significant incline (it's worth the extra effort to get up quicker), I almost miss the entrance, it is so small and unobtrusive. The road is single track between hedges that are close in on each side. There is no room for motor vehicles to pass, cars don't seem to be encouraged to come, and consequently they don't seem to use it. Grass grows in the middle, broken twigs lie scattered on the road surface, and the grass from the verges encroaches on the tarmac. Give it a few more years and the road could be gone altogether. I am cheered by the thought.

A man walking his dog encounters me, and I encounter him. We swap greetings of a familiar kind. A little further on I see that I am catching up with an older man out for a stroll. He is oblivious to my presence. I imagine him walking along here every day for the last ten years and never encountering anything or anyone apart from his mate with the dog. Hoping to avoid shocking him by suddenly appearing at his shoulder, I call out 'Morning'. He turns round suddenly, looking very startled. I have clearly failed in my objective. 'Eh, you gave me a right shock,' he says, with, however, no discernible criticism, 'I never see anyone down here. Leastways, not on a bike.'

Voice

My little lane emerges into the middle of Hellifield from behind a pub. I negotiate a very short stretch of main road. I make a short detour via an old council estate with a wonderfully generous green in the middle of a rectangle of houses. Then I'm safely on to the minor road that I'm fairly confident will take me onwards in relatively traffic-free conditions.

I cross over the railway again. There are no trains. The road too is quiet. I feel myself relax after the recent survival tensions of the main roads. The sun is still shining. The rain is still not raining.

In these moments of peace, I remember the theme of my journey, and feel my awareness reconnect with my internal world. A voice in there is reminding me to be aware of my father, and myself, and the issue of grief and death. Another voice pipes up saying that that's all very well, but that you can't push these things, you have to let them happen. I find myself smiling at the mild conflict in my head, and remember Thich Nhat Hanh, a Vietnamese Buddhist monk and teacher, whose works I like. He places a lot of emphasis on smiling, especially at those parts of ourselves which we don't particularly like. Thich Nhat Hanh, known as Thay (which means 'teacher' and is pronounced 'tie') has a very distinctive voice, strongly accented, yet clear, and full of love and compassion. I think of the extraordinary distinctiveness of individual human voices, and how attuned we are to them – how we can pick out and recognise individual voices, even years after last hearing someone. In the same way that we can identify faces and link them with individuals, we can also identify individuals' voices.

This is different from being able to conjure them up internally, which is more difficult to do, and applies for most of us, I would think, to a limited, close circle. The years have passed for me, and I don't remember my father's voice. I have photographs to remind me of his appearance. I have no recordings to remind me of his voice.

I realised the strangeness of this only a few years ago, and I asked my mother about his voice - what sort of accent he had, for example. He grew up in Hull – did he have a Hull accent, and if so, how strong, and what does a Hull accent sound like anyway.

My mother was puzzled for a while, but in the end thought he didn't have much of an accent at all. He did leave home at sixteen to join the navy, going off to HMS Ganges, which was not a ship, but a shore-based training establishment for boy sailors near Ipswich. People who leave home and travel around, living in different settings often lose some of the accent they start with, especially if it is not particularly strong, or if there are strong pressures to change. We're entering here the complex territory where class, and aspiration, and regional differences, and changing attitudes to accent intersect. My mother, for example, came from a family of nine who all started life in Brampton near Carlisle. When I came to know them years later, and well after they had all moved away, some still had strong regional accents, and some, like my mother, had mostly lost them.

As I scan through the accents and voices of the people I know, I suddenly realise the oddness, and yet the familiarity, of what I'm doing. I look more carefully at what I am doing and realise I'm doing more than scanning. I'm actually searching, and I suddenly realise what I'm searching for. I'm searching for my dad's voice. I'm checking all the voices, in case one turns out to be his. I realise that I have always been checking voices in case one turns out to be his. It's deeply buried now, under years of habit and custom, but I know, in a moment of conviction, that I have always done this, since he died.

I have done it, because, in my nine year old mind, I don't really know what being dead means, and I refuse to accept that he will never come back. To keep listening for his voice is to keep faith with my love for him. To stop listening for his voice would be a betrayal. What if they are all wrong, and he is around somewhere – suppose I stopped listening out, and he passed me by, and we missed each other because of that. I may have only the one chance; I must be on the lookout always.

In the turmoil of this recognition, and the deep longing and unhappiness and loneliness that it re-evokes, I start to cry. I feel a deep pity for a grieving, lost, but determined nine year old, and at the same time I become again that grieving, lost, but determined nine year old. I am cycling past a farmhouse, and tears are squeezing themselves past the tension of my screwed up eyes, and sobs are bubbling up past the tension of my tightened throat. A little way past the house, in a gateway to a field, with trees and bushes around, and on a bend in the road, I find a little privacy. I lean myself over the gate and, with my back to the road, let myself cry quietly until the spasms of grief, the rhythmic shakings in my stomach and chest, and the painfulness of it all, subside.

After a while, I push my bike on up an incline, start riding again at the top, and continue, with the railway on my right, and the hills on my left. The road comes to the Otterburn beck, and in order to cross, detours upstream to Otterburn itself, a settlement of a few houses, where a bridge crosses the watercourse. I feel the temptation to stop and explore, but mindful of time pressures, and still in an unusual emotional state, I run on, and run on.

On the other side of the bridge, my route comes downstream alongside the beck, and keeps alongside it through a sparsely populated valley, made to feel more remote, rather than less, by the railway tracks at one side.

I am still shaken by the insight, by the revelation. Even though I have set out on this journey deliberately to put myself in the way of discovery, part of me didn't really expect to find anything new. I had thought I had found out all there was to find out. My cosy conviction that the truth was settled and sorted has been broken by the force of emotion. With that one shift comes the possibility of more, and that too, is unsettling.

I immediately know the truth of what I have found out because it fits with another pattern that I know. I check out faces too. I check them out in case one of them is his. In crowded places I scan the crowds. Sitting in public places, I wait with unease, checking the routes in and out in case I see someone I know, someone specifically, hopefully, impossibly, who might be my dad.

When he died – when I was told he was dead – part of me refused to accept this as reality. While I was crying, and grieving, and operating in the world as though he were dead, I had another, secret, version of reality.

This is what I worked out. He was not dead at all, but had been taken away to a secret place where they were going to try and cure him. This was such a difficult and dangerous process that they had decided that it was better if everyone thought he was dead now – that way there would be no raised hopes to be dashed if it failed. In doing this, they were actually trying to help us and protect us. I decided my dad would have to be involved in this, but probably no-one else would be involved except the doctors. So it was no good trying to talk about this to anyone else. Everyone else was convinced he was actually dead, they would treat my idea as nonsense and try and talk me out of it, and so it was clear my secret source of hope had to remain a secret.

This secret, clever, explanation meant I could comfort myself with the thought that he was still somewhere in the world, and one day, maybe, I would see him again. And not only would I see him again, but see him how he used to be before the accident wrecked his body.

Comfort there might have been in this, but there was also suffering. The thought that he was still somewhere in the world, and yet we were kept separate, was very painful. My longing for him, for his body, for contact, for his voice, was at times very intense. And because it was all bound up with my secret knowledge, there was no-one I could go to for help with it. Instead I had to bear my secret knowledge alone, for I had to be watchful at all times, in case he came back.

As time passed and he did not return, I worked out a reason for this, too. He might have lost his memory through the difficult process of being made better, of being cured. Or he might have lost touch with us in some other way. He might be searching for us now, and not know how to find us. I had to scan faces, and listen to voices, and be ready to recognise him when we met. My secret knowledge also became my secret responsibility

As more time passed, the scanning process became more deeply buried in my being, covered over with other actions, or deflected into other searching processes. The years passed, the trees dropped their leaves, and the annual accumulations of leaf mould covered up what had once been on the surface.

But underneath it was still operating. I rediscovered this in my forties, in Market Square in Lancaster. With a little time to kill, I was sitting in the sunshine. I had nothing on my mind and no-one to meet, and ought to have been relaxed. Yet I noticed myself periodically glancing up and checking the people, checking the entrances to the square to see who came in. I got interested in this process and looked at it more carefully. In one of those moments of insight I was able to see how 'normal' this was for me, and yet how strange this might be for someone else. What was I doing? I realised I was checking and searching for someone, and in the next moment I realised that I was searching for my dad, and I realised also that I had always done this. In shopping malls, in pubs, in the streets. Anywhere I came across strangers, a little unconscious part of me was checking for my dad.

And now I knew that as well as looking out for him, I was also listening out for him.

Bliss

The road crosses to the other bank of the beck on a little stone-built bridge, and on the far side I pause to examine my surroundings. The beck runs close to the road with a wire fence to separate them. The beck is well up, because small trees grow from the edge of the water rather than the bank. Other evidence shows that it is not as well up as it has been. The wire fence is draped with the residue of the beck in spate: a mat of old brown and grey grasses and twigs woven into the fabric of the fence all along its bottom edge. By the beck, a young ash tree carries a decoration of the same material for the first two or three feet of its trunk. At times this road must surely be flooded, although not today.

I move on. The road is narrow, with fences rather than hedges or walls on each side. This provides a sense of space, which is accentuated when the valley opens out as I move along it. The road bends, and swoops a little up and down. With the sun shining, and the wind blowing me along strongly from behind, I make fast progress, almost effortlessly. The straighter I sit up, the more the wind can act on my body as though it is a sail, and the straighter I sit up, then the more clearly I can see and enjoy my surroundings. It is blissful riding, my fingertips lightly on the handlebars to give the gentlest of guidance, while my legs easily turn the biggest gear, and slight sways of my bodyweight preserve the improbable, the miraculous, balance of a bicycle at speed.

The strength of the wind has another unlikely gift to offer: quiet. I am travelling at speed, but without the wind rushing in my ears. Because the wind speed and my speed are about equal, then I cycle in relative silence: effortless, peaceful, silent speed. At this moment, with this amount of pleasure, I am deeply grateful to be alive and in a precious human body that can feel.

On the tracks alongside me, a train appears. With EWS printed in large letters on its side, the two units, and the three carriages, clank their way north-west, heading probably for Carlisle. Their sheer metallic bulk and power seem alien to this isolated rural valley, and alien to the human-scale emotional physicality that I am experiencing.

Unlike the train, I have choices to make in my route, and the possibility of going astray. I must pay close attention to my map, and relate it to the ground, as I have to make choices at two or three junctions in near proximity. I am downsizing, for the next couple of miles, from minor road to track, and I need to make sure I'm going the right way. A few yards down my chosen track, a bridge over the river Aire, which here is a small early version of its later grand self, confirms I am heading in the right direction.

I am looking forward to this next bit. In my forward planning for the journey, I had roughed out a route on my maps. As part of my aim of minimising traffic contact, I had highlighted any officially designated cycleways. Most of these are no more than signposts pointing down minor roads, the sort of routes anyone could work out for themselves (although occasionally they do have the advantage of improved junctions at, or crossings of, major roads). But some cycleways are more valuable. These are the genuine off-road, traffic-free routes, and in my experience, worth cycling quite a long way to get to (well, a mile or two anyway). Disused railway tracks make excellent cycle tracks. They are flat. Canal towpaths ditto.

But other parts of the network of human-scale routes across our country can be hauled into the frame and adapted for cycle use. Principal among these are tracks and bridleways. You can walk on a public footpath, but you cannot ride your horse (or your bike) on one. You can however ride your horse on a public bridleway, and you can ride your trusty metal steed on one too. With a little gravel, or cinders, or some such, laid down, a bridleway makes a perfectly serviceable cycle track. The main inconvenience is occasional lumbering equine obstacles, and the deep indentations their shod feet make in the surface, but, hey, who needs perfection?

At some point in my research I had highlighted the bridleway I am about to travel. Or rather, I distinctly remember seeing it highlighted on one of my maps, though, to tell the truth, not the one I am currently using. I am therefore convinced that it is some kind of official regional cycle route, and will have had official attention paid to it. Anyway, the route is there, it takes me in the direction I want to go, and it will certainly get me away from any traffic. In my longing for comfort, I imagine an easy ride over an even surface.

The track, for the time being, remains tarmacked as it eases its way past several dwellings. The tarmacked track ends at a recently modernised dwelling that blocks my way, and says quite clearly, 'No further down this way, mate.' To my left, up a hill, is a very rough farm track: stony, rutted, grass growing in the middle, little streams of water flowing down each rut, dry stone walled on each side. Now this is your track, mate.

In its own way, it is a classic farm track, and very beautiful too. But it does not fit in with my preconceptions of what it should be like, and I am, therefore, though loathe to admit this, just a little disappointed.

Rough

I pause to take stock of my situation. I lean my bike against a convenient wall. I try to look suitably innocent so that the owners of the dwelling, if they are in, and if they notice my presence, and if they are at all interested in my presence (all of which I doubt), do not think that I am lurking here in order to case their joint for a later burglary. As I have actually been accused of this very thing by a paranoid owner in the past, I am myself not being entirely paranoid here.

A glance at the map reveals an alternative route - a longer way round by road, which would guarantee smooth riding. However it would mean retracing my route a little. I convince myself that the track might get better further on. I don't take much convincing. I'm a sucker for the kind of argument that says, 'You don't have to decide anything, you'll be fine, just keep going'.

I keep going, which in this case involves pushing my heavily laden bike up the rough track, a considerably more onerous proposition than pushing it up a nice smooth tarmac surface. The incline leads to a near horizon, beyond which I cannot see, so I do not know how the track develops. Does it improve, or does it deteriorate? When I get to the top of the slope, I see that the track stretches further up the hill, at a lesser incline, till it reaches a corner. There it turns right to contour along the side of the hill. I can see its course. I can also see its condition: rough and ready, the same as before. More pushing for me then.

While the condition of the track remains the same, my condition does not. With the sun now shining brightly, and considerable effort being expended, I get hotter. I therefore remove the overtrousers that I put on just before leaving this morning. As is the usual way in these circumstances, that event seems an awfully long time ago, at least a quarter of a life time. Under my overtrousers, my undertrousers remain free of damp and condensation. I am agreeably surprised. The product seems to have done just what it says on the blurb.

I push on, trying to steer a route that avoids the largest stones. I need to minimise the jolting to my wheels, especially the back one where the main burden of my baggage rests. Occasionally I suffer the occupational hazard of the bike pusher. This is when, despite your best efforts to avoid it, the pedal catches your ankle, usually right on the bony bit that sticks out, and causes that instant neurological response commonly known as pain. I console myself with the thought that at least I'm not now in any danger of tearing my new, and efficient, overtrousers.

When the track reaches the corner and turns right, it stops being a track. The tractors that use it and therefore keep it track-like seem to head off into the fields at this point. I am left with what can only be described as a footpath. It has been a track, because the width is still there between wall and fence, and the stony surface is still there to make bike riding very awkward. But the grass has grown over from the verges to leave only a narrow path in the middle, and on each side the hawthorns and hazels and elders are crowding in to make passage more difficult, more sheltered, more natural.

One day, if I live long enough, and technology changes, I may, after it has fallen into disuse, see a similar process taking place on the M6. Now that would be fun.

I tentatively try riding. I decide that if I go very slowly in bottom gear I can steer between the worst of the stones, and that I can also shift my bodyweight around so that it doesn't all sag on to my vulnerable back wheel. I'm aware that a sticker on the bike when I bought it said it wasn't designed for off road stuff, or some such. I'm also aware that the back wheel isn't quite true, and I had to ease off the brakes when I was preparing for the trip in order to stop the wheel sticking on them. A weakness there could be amplified by the undue strain imposed by jolting up and down on stones with the weight of heavy panniers and me on it. A buckled back wheel would not be an aid to progress.

It all adds up to a strong case for walking, but I keep riding anyway. A whiney voice arises in my head to argue the case for riding: I'm being careful, aren't I? And my legs ache and I need to sit down on my comfy saddle. Leave me alone, you sensible bully.

Riding my bike, even at a slow pace over stony ground, feels like what I'm meant to do, but anxiety still grips me. What if I really do wreck the back wheel? Won't I be in trouble?

After wrestling with this one for a while, I realise I'm grappling with internal authority here. What I'm most worried about is breaking the rules set by the message on my bike when I bought it. That's the trouble I might get into. After I remind myself that I'm quite a big man now, and that if the wheel breaks, then that's my affair, and I have enough money in the bank to buy another one, then the anxiety eases away. In fact the whole bike belongs to me, I tell myself, and if I want to wreck it, or give it away, or leave it by the side of this footpath, walk off, and never see it again, then that is entirely up to me, and nobody else can interfere. That feels better.

However, a wrecked back wheel, or a wrecked bike, would be inconvenient to the purpose of my journey, so when the track starts to go downhill, and larger stones start to appear, I do the sensible thing, and get off and walk, and push.

After a particularly rocky section, where the track, going downhill between banks lined with overhanging trees, feels more like a river bed than a thoroughfare, the quality of the surface changes once more. Compacted soil and mud provides a more even surface, and I ride again, with relief. A series of large puddles across the path challenges my steering and balance, and then, alongside a wood with mature trees, the path changes back to track, and then the track changes back to road with metalled surface. I have made it to the other side.

Starved

The road is high enough above the surrounding country to afford a generous view across fields and river and villages fading into the distance. Freewheeling slowly down the gentle incline, I switch my attention between road and view.

A footpath sign on the left points to where the Pennine Way diverges from this road to head further northwest, roughly the way I have just come. I see the ghost of myself, walking up this road twenty-seven years ago, on my way to the hostel at Malham, after sleeping out under the stars a couple of nights before. At Malham I will buy my first pair of thick woollen socks, and discover that they make a significant difference to my comfort. Do I always find things out the hard way?

Ahead of me, in the distance and moving left across my field of vision, I see three exotic creatures. They are red in colour, and moving so rapidly that at first I take them for deer. Then they resolve into something more civilised. They are cyclists – proper cyclists – dressed in all the gear, and cycling seriously fast along a road at right angles to mine.

I cross over a canal, the Leeds and Liverpool, which I will meet again later on. And with that I am in Gargrave, a picturesque little settlement enhanced by the river, the railway, and the canal, but overwhelmed by the heavy traffic of the A65 right through its centre. I have, I confess, been a contributor to that heavy traffic on numerous occasions. From the comfort of my car on those occasions, I have noticed a café frequented by cyclists, their machines lined up outside in serried ranks. I have an idea that I might join them, and partake of cyclist-style refreshment, even if I am not wearing the de rigeur fluorescent skin-tight cycling accoutrements. Alas, when I get there, it is to discover that the establishment is closed on Mondays, no doubt to enable recovery from the hordes of weekend cyclists. I must retrace my steps (or, more accurately, wheel circumferences) to another hostelry a little further back along the side road I have just come down.

I look at the menu outside. As ever, I am hopeful of mouth-watering and nutritious fare. However, as I have an awkward diet (no meat, no dairy, no sugar, and no tea or coffee) it is somewhat of a forlorn hope, and indeed here, as usual, I am disappointed. I stand and waver. Why can't I just eat the normal stuff, like everyone else, and have an easy café life? But I don't, so I'm faced with a familiar dilemma. To stay pure and cycle on, or to compromise and go in? I'm in holiday mood, so in it is. Several windows give me a clear view of the interior, which shows space available, and reassures me in my anxiety at entering strange establishments.

I chain my bike to a drainpipe, get my valuables from the saddlebag, and go in. It is late morning.

Inside, it is quite genteel, and in my trainers, and clutching various plastic bags containing valuables like my overtrousers, I do not feel that I quite match up. Still, the proprietor's not in the room, so I get sat down quickly before he can come in and order me out. When he does come in, he is of course perfectly friendly, and I do the ordering. I go for Assam tea and lemon, plus a teacake.

A foreign couple is at one table. Another couple of couples come in, separately, shortly after. Their accents give clues to their origins. One set are holidaymakers from the south east. Apart from ordering, they sit together in silence. It's not a particularly comfortable silence. The older couple are local, the man's accent stronger than his wife's. They chat on unconcernedly about various domestic issues.

The tea, coupled with the warmth of the room, makes me hot. I remove my jacket, and my fleece, and add them to my collection of plastic bags, so that the space around me is littered with my belongings. I busy myself with my maps, checking the route to come.

The voices around me remind me of my insight into the search for my dad, and listening out for his voice. I find myself smiling when I think of him, and smiling when I think of my three children, and of Mary. These are my main people, the ones around whom most of the love in my life is focussed and exchanged.

I wonder whether, in my search for my dad, it was his individual voice that was most important, or the quality of love in it. Was what I was missing that delight in who I was, the unconditional regard, that I think my father brought to me? I think of Mary's voice and how it may contain love, or how love may be less apparent, through tiredness or other reasons. My own voice to other people must be similarly variable. It is not hard to allow a little more love to show, and I resolve to practice showing more love in my voice. I think of the anecdotes I've heard of orphan babies after the Second World War, provided with the necessities of life in orphanages, but starved of loving contact. The survival rate was not high. Love can be a matter of life and death, especially at a young age.

Dip

I exit the teashop, and Gargrave. I cross over the river, go past the church, and over the railway. At this stage I'm heading due south, the sun is shining almost warmly, and the wind has lessened to a stiff breeze. As is often the case after a lengthy stop, I am surprised by how quickly, on a bike, I can move under my own power. It's as though my body has forgotten, and reverted to normal awareness: no powered transport equals walking equals slow.

Within a few minutes, however, I have stopped riding and started pushing as I come to a steep climb. Part way up, hearing my breathing getting heavier, and feeling the extra strain in my chest, I start to feel the stress of the climb, and want it to be over. As it will not be over till I am at the top, some way off yet, I also start to get anxious and bored, which in me are often quite closely related.

With my laboured breathing so much at the forefront of my awareness though, I am able to remember Thay's (Thich Nhat Hanh's) advice on returning to an awareness of the self. It is to repeat this phrase: breathing in, I know I am breathing in, breathing out, I know I am breathing out. As usual, within a few breaths I feel calmer, and more focussed in the moment. He says it takes only three breaths, done with awareness, to bring yourself back to yourself, and away from the distractions that lead to suffering.

I find myself smiling, and enjoying the views opening out behind me, and as I reach the top of the climb, in front of me too. Behind me is the territory I have traversed today. Gargrave is nestled, as all picturesque villages should be nestled, in a fold in the surrounding rolling countryside. The dark green trees of autumn point up the shining green of the fields, and beyond the fields, forming the horizon, lie the hills and fells of the Pennines. Over all, the arching dome of the sky is composed of the shifting grey cloud cover that fits very well with an equinoctial day. In front is Glusburn Moor, where I am headed. This is actual new territory for me; I have never been on these roads before. Smooth, rounded hills are near me, one with a mast on top.

I review my progress briefly, and feel reasonably confident, given how far I've travelled, that I'm on track to make it to my stop for the night. Paying attention to my parallel inner journey, I decide that is also progressing reasonably well. I have now remembered to pay attention to my breathing, and if I can continue to do that, then the opportunities of the moment will remain more available to me. I have remembered that love is important, and if I can love myself, then at least someone is doing it. I laugh at this, and move on, swooping wonderfully down a steep, broad descent into a dip, and making it part way up the other side with the speed of my momentum, before having to concede to the force of gravity, and get off and walk again.

Matchbox

Riding once more, I find myself thinking of my early cycling experiences. I got my first two-wheeler on my eighth birthday, a single speed bike, bought second hand. It was collected from some distance away and then ridden home, I was told, by my Uncle Jim. He would have been way too big for it, so there was an act of devotion.

With the arrival of that bike in my life, my horizons expanded, and I cycled round the area where we lived, on the outskirts of Leeds, in a way that would not be possible now because of the increase in traffic (and fear of abduction).

In my memories, I am always cycling alone, and indeed I think that is how it was. I did have friends, and we did play together at home, and we also played out, mostly down by the beck. But I do not recall any of my friends having bikes, or going out on bikes with me. So at this time what I see is a small boy cycling round the streets and lanes on his own.

Some of this was exploring. I was curious and wanted to see the way the world looked outside my familiar home zone.

And some of this was collecting. After bonfire night I would go out the next day and see how many used rockets I could find, and bring them back home, and keep them, sometimes in conjunction with my brother.

And I developed a hobby of matchbox collecting. When I had collected them, I had a big scrapbook that I stuck them in. I got hold of them by cycling round the area with my eyes in the gutter and spotting them, lying where they had been thrown away by passers-by. The excitement of finding a new one, an unusual one, was very satisfying. The common ones – there was one with a blue Scottish thistle on – were irritatingly common. I learned that there were more to be found on main roads than on side streets, so I must have had some concept of traffic. Well-meaning relatives, who perhaps found my hobby a little strange, but indulged me anyway, sometimes provided me with samples from pubs or hotels they'd been to. While I accepted these, they didn't really satisfy me: I wanted to find them myself, by looking.

As I cycle along now, an adult alone, I am filled with compassion for a small boy, making his way and surviving as best he can in a strange world over which he has so little control. I see him as lonely, without friends who really understand, and I feel my own loneliness at this moment. I see him searching for his lost father, lost even while he was still alive, because the man in the wheelchair could not play with him, or be the companion that he had been once. And I see him searching for his lost father, doubly lost when he died. Doubly lost because he was gone, and yet might not be gone, might himself be wandering lost in the world, looking for his family, looking for his son.

And then I find myself crying again, and the tears welling up from my eyes blur my vision, and I must stop at the side of the road, and blow my nose, and hope that no cars come by to see my distress.

And when I turn right on to a main road a few minutes later, I am still sniffling, and feeling vulnerable among the fast moving traffic. It is a relief to turn off almost straight away, and cross a bridge among woods high over a river, and so be further on my way.

Closed

It is now really, really windy again. The sound of the wind gusting in the trees around me is unsettling. There is some relief for me in concentrating on the practicalities of movement, and progress, and effort.

A little further on I have to pause to check my route outside an estate – one of those country houses that has been turned into offices, with a noticeboard telling you which organisations are located there, and a driveway disappearing behind bushes so that the main house remains hidden. I'm not feeling brave enough, or curious enough to venture a look, and instead push my bike on up the hill. After a bit of an effort, the road takes me past the back entrance, the tradesmen's entrance. Here I feel much more comfortable. I know my place.

Just past here the road is blocked by a notice that says 'Road Closed at School.' I panic mildly at this. I don't want to have to go back where I've come, considering the effort it's taken to get here. I know I am panicking, because I am desperate enough to look around for someone to ask whether it's really blocked. In fact a woman in a car emerges from a nearby driveway at that very moment, but luckily by this time my panic has already passed, and therefore I don't have to try and flag her down, and possibly fail, which would be embarrassing.

Instead, I decide to risk it. After all, I realise, I am on a bike, not in a car. Even if the road is completely blocked by road works, all I have to do is lift my bike into the field alongside, and go through the field till the road works are past. I have a (relatively) light-weight flexible friend.

I progress along a pleasant, narrow country lane, expecting to come across a blocked road round every bend. I see a building that might have been an old school. I see some men that might be builders although they are currently on a break. I see a disused railway line from the bridge that crosses over it. I fail to see the Roman road marked on the map, but perhaps I'm not paying close enough attention. I continue to fail to see any road closure. I do see, when I reach the next road junction, a companion sign to the one I passed a mile back, warning me that the road I have just come along is closed at the school.

The hamlet where I am is at a crossroads. The map tells me that a little further down one of the arms of the cross not on my route, there is a hall, a castle, and a Roman fort. As this seems a particularly rich feast for a tiny settlement, I decide to waste some energy and explore. I pass a stone wall that might belong to a hall. Of fort or castle there is no sign, the road starts to descend, and I decide I don't have that amount of energy to waste, and head back. Closer examination of the map suggests Burwen Castle and the Roman fort are probably one and the same thing.

On a little triangle of grass in the middle of this place, sheltered by the overhanging branches of a tree, I see a curious thing. Ten large wedge shaped stones have been placed in a particular arrangement: one on end followed by a pile of two, a pile of four, another pile of two, and another on end at the other end. Why?

It does not look useful to me, and nor, really, does it look particularly artistic. It does look mildly eccentric. Perhaps that is reason enough to exist in the world. Not that any reason, actually, is required.

Counting

My route out takes me uphill, at first in a shaded little valley where the road runs next to a stream. Later I progress to the open hillside. Whatever the surroundings, the road continues relentlessly upwards and I, consequently, continue to walk, and push relentlessly. I am now also regretting the pot of tea I had earlier, as I can feel the effects - effects I recognise from previous experience: an empty, gnawing sensation in my stomach, low energy levels, and a lot of sweating.

As I grind up the hill, forgetting to breathe and feel cheerful a la Thich Nhat Hanh, I find a song going round and round in my head. Appropriately enough this is 'The Circle Song': '...like a circle in a circle, like a wheel within a wheel, never ending or beginning on an ever spinning...' Or some such wording of my own re-creation. At first this is a pleasant distraction, but later, stuck inside the ever spinning, the pleasure begins to pall. Even my usual trick - replacing one obsessive song with another obsessive but different song – fails to work.

I ponder the nature of my obsessions. Last night at home, I listened to Mary talking on the phone to our son Robbie. The conversation had moved into an area where they were discussing people's coping mechanisms, how they manage in difficult circumstances, how they channel their anxieties and fears. She was telling him that one of my responses to my dad's death was to get into counting. I would, while lying in bed at night before going to sleep, count repetitive movements of my fingers and toes. I would clench my hands slightly and count ten. I would clench them again slightly and count twenty. If I clenched my feet as well, I could count twenty at a time. I don't remember how many I counted to. During the day, at times, I would count slight grinding motions of my teeth.

Later on I developed a project. I went through the bible noting the number of verses in each chapter, and added them up.

I also went through the house finding all the 'made in Britain' marks on objects, and adding them up on a room by room basis. The kitchen was the best because of all the marks on the bottom of the pottery.

As an adult now, it's quite easy to describe these behaviours as obsessive coping actions, tying down the energy of anxiety, or grief, which would otherwise be too difficult to handle. At the time, they were just what I did. They made it possible for me to get by and survive. Well done me. I did it.

It's not difficult to guess that as a child I was afraid of death, and dying. I also had good reasons to fear being injured, and being left helpless. Going to sleep was a particularly difficult time. To sleep perchance to dream, ay, there's the rub.

In one vivid nightmare, I was kept prisoner with others in a large house that had the atmosphere of a laboratory. In the house, from time to time, people were strapped into special chairs, like dentists chairs, and made to grow. Once they grew to ten feet tall, they would die.

I was very afraid in this dream, and afraid when I woke up, and I have been at least a little afraid every time I have thought of it since.

If I ignore the fear, and the nightmarish qualities for a while, it's actually a very good dream, creatively bringing together important aspects of my life, and giving clues to aspects that are less fully in awareness. The laboratory speaks of mysterious doctors, and the control they seem to have over people's lives. As a child, I know only that they have power. I do not know the limits of that power. Perhaps they, or adults like them, can really make people grow. Perhaps they can cure my father in the secret place that I think he might be in. If he is being held secretly, then perhaps that it is not a pleasant experience. Maybe it is secret because the process is so horrible – maybe it is more akin to torture, maybe he is suffering.

But there is already distress in his and my lives. Being strapped in a chair is a close equivalent to the kind of physical helplessness that I have observed my dad experience for over three years. He is put in a wheelchair; he cannot move himself; he cannot get out of the wheelchair himself.

At the same time the dream says that this experience is something I fear could happen to me. I may become helpless like him. I will grow older, and bigger, and the dream tells me I will die – not when I'm old, but as soon as I reach a certain size. The size that makes sense in this context is adult size. The dream suggests that I was scared of growing up to be a man, because the fate that awaited me was that which had befallen my father.

Where there is a void of unknowing, our imaginations will tend to fill it with whatever fits, and sometimes that can be worse than the truth. I had a large void of unknowing around death, and I filled it with my private creations. Now I am an adult, I still have a void of unknowing about death, but I have mostly filled it with the world's creations.

Dripping

Near the top of the grind, I see a crossroads just ahead of me. On my right is a coniferous wood, with a stone wall alongside the road, and a muddy patch where in the past cars have pulled off into an unofficial lay-by. There are no cars today and so there is plenty of room for me and my bike. I pull over and sit with my back to the wall. The wind is still up, and the wall, and the wood, provide some shelter. There are dark grey clouds scudding low overhead, and spittings of moisture in the air. All the signs point to an imminent downpour, and I want to get some rest in, and some food in, before it starts.

Though my nibblings are very welcome, and the weight off my feet also welcome, my immediate surroundings are less so. Copious quantities of plastic rubbish are strewn around, much of it caught in various obstructions and therefore reluctant to be blown away. Thanks, vehicle drivers, for your skilled creation of full-on horribleness.

Across the road however, I see and admire some long, tall, brown grasses, very attractive in their dried up autumn guise, bending gently in unison before the gusts of wind. Thanks, evolution.

The rain holds off, and I get some rest, but not quite enough before I start to feel cold again, and am driven to get moving. I grab a final quick glance at the map. The grind up the hill has been so tiring that I know I made an error on my route selection. I should have taken a slightly longer but flatter route. I can still re-join this alternative, but that means turning left at the crossroads ahead and losing height rapidly again. That goes against the grain. If I continue, I have some more climbing to do, but the question is how much. How close are those contour lines? I decide to go on, straight ahead.

There is a little climb, but it is fairly gentle, and I manage to ride it. Then I find myself on a plateau, the road undulating as I make my way under the darkening sky, with fields on one side, and moorland on the other. I make it to the far edge, start to drop down, and am part way through a long wonderful freewheel, when the rain starts to come down hard, and I must stop to put on my overtrousers and pull up my hood.

Setting off again, I find the rain driving into my side, and the wind buffeting me with its hearty gusts, and I am forced to go softly for safety's sake.

Just past a crossroads, I spot a cyclist coming towards me. He seems to be the first one I can remember meeting today. I wave to him, and call out greetings. He responds, and then on an impulse, I swirl my bike round and join him on the other side. He is an old man, quite little, pushing his bike along into the teeth of the rain and driving wind. Three or four bags of shopping are hung from the handlebars of his bike, an old green one with a chainguard. He wears a flat cap, but his face is exposed, and the rain is dripping off it from every aspect. His face is very weather-beaten, he has some teeth missing, and his eyes look in slightly different directions. They are also very bloodshot. On his exposed neck, white hair grows where he has not shaved it off.

I ask if he has far to go till he gets home. He speaks very low, so that I have to lean a little closer to make sure I hear him. 'Not so far,' he says, 'not so far to go now.' He says he goes shopping 'two or three times a week, mebbe.' I get the feeling he lives alone, and hope he will be able to get warm and dry when he gets in. He asks me where I'm going. I tell him I'm going to stay with my brother at Eldwick. He asks me if it is near……?

The wind is strong, and I don't hear the name of the place, which I probably wouldn't know anyway. I say I'm not sure. 'Is it on the top?' he asks, and I can confirm that it is on the top, near Bingley. We seem to think we are talking about the same place, and that seems to make us happy. We are trying to communicate with each under difficult circumstances. I feel a ready affection for him, but I also feel respect for an old guy still going strong in a world that for him remains physically tough. Perhaps he can detect this as we seem to have goodwill for each other. We chat on a little more, but it is hard to ignore the weather, and I have also stopped with my bike well out into the road. This means the occasional passing car is temporarily inconvenienced, but it is also means it is not particularly safe for me. So we say goodbye, and pass on our way.

Monsters

Within a few minutes, the rain eases, and stops. The sun comes out and the day, and the landscape around, transforms. The way ahead descends, ever steeper, down once more into the valley of the Aire. I lose all the rest of the height I have so painfully won in one glorious charge into civilisation below. Moors fall behind, fields disappear; houses and Glusburn appear. It is odd to experience the rapidity of the change. I am suddenly appearing in a strange settlement where people live their lives today, and where generations have lived their lives in the past. I flit through, scarcely noticed, a ghost on a bike.

I hit a main road, and become less ghost-like and more noticeable, I hope, to the drivers trying to get past me. The temptation as a cyclist in these circumstances is to try and squeeze yourself and your bike into the gutter to get away from the monsters eager to get on and get past you. This is an error. The monsters take this as a sign of weakness and puniness, and bully their way through the gap as though you don't exist. You are squeezed even more, and left with no more gutter to hide in. What you actually have to do, if you want to improve your survival chances, is to stick yourself out into the road, make them notice you, and make them take positive overtaking action. They have to pull out to get past you, and most of them only do that when it's safe to do so (from their point of view). Some of course, will insist on pulling out when it's not safe to do so. And what do they do then, when they discover themselves in the middle of the road with a heavyweight lorry, say, bearing down rapidly towards them?

They make the following rapid calculation. If I continue on my present course, I will die in a tangled mass of shattered metal and glass following an unpleasant collision. However, if I pull sharply to the left, like this… I will save myself. Phew, that was close. I wonder what's for tea tonight. Oh, was there a cyclist or something back there?

Yes, you are the cyclist or something back there, but you have survived, because you gave yourself plenty of gutter room to move in. You have also survived because you have got your defensive swerving and breaking action in first. You have not trusted those motorised purveyors of mayhem an inch. You have been warned.

I navigate the dangers of a railway level crossing, and avoid getting my wheel stuck in the tracks as a train bears down on me. I navigate successfully the dangers of a large roundabout, choosing a relatively traffic free period, sticking myself centrally in my lane (see warning, above), and signalling vigorously when I am leaving it.

I cross the Aire and head uphill once more on a thankfully minor road. I am in inhabited territory again, and houses, mostly old, stone-built and terraced, accompany the road. The terraces are fitted in creatively and compactly on the steep hillside, while roads and ginnels thread their way amongst them. I come to a low narrow tunnel, made to seem more claustrophobic by the walls on each side as I approach it. It is short, but I do not understand what it is for till I get out the other side, climb a little rise, and realise that I have just come under the canal.

I pause at a footbridge over the canal, and watch as a group of ducks gets in and out of the water at a kind of concrete landing area. The sunlight is glinting brightly off the water. The surface of the water is ruffled up into a regular series of little waves, driven along endlessly by the power of the wind which is blowing directly along the canal.

My route takes me diagonally up the hill so that I can gain enough height to turn sharply right at the top, and head off in my preferred direction. As I push steadily up the hill I have time to look into the windows of the terraced houses on my left, situated conveniently close to the road for this purpose. Though some are screened by net curtains, others display their interiors more openly, and I can look right through, ascertain their taste in furniture and décor, and admire the view from their rear windows, high above the dropping hillside. This view offers an uninterrupted panorama of the Aire valley and the hills and moors beyond, the territory, in fact, that I have just traversed.

Hoist

I am bowling along a minor road which contours along the hillside above the Aire valley. I have on my right a high level view across a wet landscape lit up by the bright afternoon sunshine. I pass houses that indicate I've moved into a more prosperous part of the country, perhaps because we're closer now to Leeds and Bradford. There are old farm houses done up. There are stables attached to them, and horses in the fields. There is the spectre of 'private' and 'keep out' signs. I look out for my particular favourite in terms of peculiar protection of property: 'no turning,' but I don't see one. Whatever the vibe, these are all homes to some folks.

After my dad's accident we had a strange time for the next year, because our normal home life was over. In fact after several months where my mother tried to look after us in Portsmouth, and be with dad in hospital in Aylesbury at the same time, we gave the house in Portsmouth back to the Navy. We went to stay in rooms in Aylesbury, though I went off to stay with my auntie Mary in Edinburgh for a couple of months first.

During this period in Aylesbury, other arrangements were being made in Leeds, near to where my mother's brother Jim and sister-in-law Dot lived. We were having a bungalow built. It had adaptations like sliding doors and a raised bath, so that it was suitable for use by someone in a wheelchair. The idea was that if we lived close to Dot and Jim, they'd be able to help us, which is the way it turned out.

The money for this building came partly from savings, but a substantial amount came from a big fundraising effort by the men from the PT school and other naval friends. They did events to raise money, including a football match against a showbiz XI which, on the programme at least, included a very young Sean Connery. I have also seen a list of contributions made from groups all over. I remember a group of Army PTIs had sent a donation with their best wishes. I feel very moved when I think of the effort that so many people put in to try and help. It did make a difference, because it enabled us to have a home again.

My mother was determined that we would be back together again, and that she would have her husband at home and look after him there. I can only guess at the organisational and emotional effort involved in having a bungalow built 250 miles away at the same time as supporting a paralysed husband and two young children while living in rented rooms in an era before telephones were very common. I know she got support from family and friends, particularly Dot and Jim, which must have been very important.

But I know she had also to face many things alone. She has told me how she would normally visit dad in hospital during the day, but also in the evening after we were asleep. The woman where we boarded would listen out for us children, but my mother had made a rule for herself that she wouldn't leave us till we were asleep. Sometimes that would take a long time, as these things do, and she knew then that my dad would be fretting. She would rush to the hospital, where he would be waiting anxiously to see her, and be upset that she was late, even though, of course, he knew why.

My main awareness of things happening on the housing front was the excitement of three or four very heavy parcels arriving through the post one day. These were boxes containing different coloured bricks, so we could choose which ones the bungalow would be built out of. After due serious consideration we chose a light sandy colour.

In late 1959, we moved into the bungalow, though it wasn't quite finished, and workmen were still treading through the kitchen in their muddy boots while my mother tried to get things clean and in good order. My brother and I went off to school in Ireland Wood for three weeks till the Christmas holidays. It was a very short stay at this school, because a new one nearer to home was opening after Christmas. It was my brother's first schooling. He was just short of five, and I was seven and a half. We travelled there each day on a bus, a Leeds double-decker, unaccompanied by anyone apart from a few other children also going to that school.

Shortly before Christmas, about thirteen months after he left home in Portsmouth and never returned, my dad came back to live with us, brought in an ambulance, and we were all together again. We had two years to go.

Aspects of our life there return to me, particularly those involving my father. He had to be looked after completely. He did have movement of his head, and his speech and mental faculties were unaffected. He also had a very limited movement of his right arm, but that is all. Various attempts had been made by the hospital to utilise the arm movement so that he could do the odd thing for himself. For example, they had made a frame which could be strapped to his wrist, with a long metal rod emerging vertically from the top. Attached to this was a cigarette holder. If someone stuck a cigarette in it, and lit it, he could raise and lower his forearm just enough to enable him to take some puffs. There are photographs of him trying this out in the hospital, surrounded by clouds of smoke. I think at home we just put a lighted cigarette in his mouth and took it out briefly when it needed the ash knocking off the end. I think I remember doing this, though I am not certain.

I am clear about other things I did for him. I manoeuvred him round the house in his wheelchair. When his feet fell off the footrests of the chair, I lifted his feet, feeling the weight of his legs also, and put them back on. On his feet there were a particular pair of brown leather slippers. They never wore out.

In order to move him between bed and chair, we had a hydraulic hoist to help. He would be lying on the bed on top of a hammock-type thing, with metal rings at the edge. We would wheel the hoist to the bed so that the arm of the hoist was above him, and attach cords between the rings and the arm. Then we would pump with a handle, and, very gradually, he would start to rise. In some way, probably to do with the arrangement of the cords, he came up into a sitting position, suspended in the hammock beneath the hoist arm. Then we would swing him round until he was above the wheelchair. In order to lower him, we had to twist a small round knob that released the pressure in the hydraulic system so that he descended. The crucial thing was to do this slowly, otherwise the pressure came off too suddenly and he dropped with a jerk. Once he was in the chair the cords could be released, and he was ready to be moved to the living room, or the kitchen, or the garden for the next part of his day.

I remember pumping that hoist and seeing him rise. I remember swinging him round, his heavy body manageable by me through the agency of the technology. And I remember dropping him carefully down into his chair.

Diaries

I find myself dropping down into Silsden. Just outside the centre, I detour into some streets at the side to look at a small area of compact terraces – frontages straight on to the streets, walled-in yards at the back. Some are for sale, and, interested like most of our property-owning democracy in the going rate for houses, I wonder idly if there are any bargains to be had here.

A little further down the hill, there is a terrace end-on to the road with a beck emerging from a tunnel underneath it at the gable end. As far as I can tell, it's a whole terrace built over a beck – well, that's one way to find a vacant building plot.

The weather has gone cold and wet again, with the wind chill factor increasing. I wander the streets a little, wondering what I might find. I notice some shops, but, with the weather as it is, few shoppers. An estate agent's window reveals to me that no, even for basic terraced houses in Silsden, there are no bargains to be had. A couple of people wait hunched up at a bus stop. In a car park I spot a gents toilet and wander over to take advantage. (Rule one for men of a certain age: never pass up the opportunity for a pee - Billy Connolly.) I leave my bike in the entrance passage for safety. When I return, the rain has intensified, and I stand and watch from my shelter. As it shows no sign of abating, I decide to hang out here for a while. Hanging out in public toilets is not usually my style, but, I reassure myself, I'm in the lobby rather than the main body. It's just a convenient place to shelter from the rain, anyone can see that. The rain is keeping other potential users away in fact; there is no-one else within sight. It is actually reasonably warm in here after the unwelcome attentions of the wind, and, while I'm relatively comfortable, I make the most of the situation and have a snack too.

All good things come to an end, the rain eases off, and I head off. Descending further down the central street, I see a lot more shops, and more people. I find myself level with the canal again, because the road crosses over it, and I stop to look, as fascinated as ever by the historical equivalent of a motorway. I see canal boats, and what look like the remains of old warehouses. I wonder how much of Silsden's reason for being here has to do with the coming of the canal as a bringer of trade possibilities and prosperity – prosperity for some anyway.

My intended route will take me along parallel to the canal, but at a higher level, so I have first to gain height. On the map this ascent is evidenced by some contour lines disturbingly close together, but it looks like it will be a short sharp shock, so I figure I'll just get it over with quick, and then chill out on a high level ride.

On the outskirts of Silsden, with my climb in view ahead, I pause for a rest. I sit in the sunshine on the pavement outside the entrance gates to a cemetery, my back to the wall. An old man passes me, and enters, but we do not exchange greetings. I assume he is visiting a grave, perhaps his wife's.

I check my mobile phone and there is a message from my son Ewan asking me to ring him. As my battery is very low, I text him to say I'll ring him this evening, and switch it off again.

My father was cremated, so there is no grave for me to visit. Before the funeral that I didn't go to, there came the news that changed everything. He had gone back to Stoke Mandeville for a check-up after Christmas. We were expecting him to return in a few days. On New Year's morning, my mother came into the room that my brother and I shared. We were in our bunk beds. She slid back the sliding door, and came into the room holding a diary in each hand. She always gave us a diary as a present on New Year's Day. She held out the little diaries in each hand, and looked at us with her soft brown eyes, and a little smile. 'I have some rather bad news,' she said, and told us. I began crying and it felt like I could never stop.

I recall her helping me, after a while, into the living room. I am still in my pyjamas. He is still dead. I am trying to eat my breakfast. A bowl of Weetabix is resting on the flat arm of our armchair. The covering is a bright blue colour. I am crying into my Weetabix. I feel sick and ill. I am nine and a half, and he was forty.

Phonecall

From where I am sitting, the road that I need to get to is plainly visible as a line along the edge of the hillside ahead of me. It rises disconcertingly high above me in an unpleasantly short distance. That could spell trouble. The old man who had passed me earlier going into the cemetery, passes me coming out. It's time to move, and I mount and ride on.

The road ahead of me is easy to start with, and I'm pleased to be back in amongst the fields and hedgerows, and out of town. The sun is shining. It's a great afternoon. Then the road starts to rise, and rise, and rise. And I push, and push, and rest, and rest, and push some more. It has spelt trouble.

I feel like a peasant, trudging on under a relentless burden. I try to remember to breathe, and focus on the moment, but I can't make it work. It's just all too trudgey. Even conjuring up images of Vietnamese

Buddhist peasants trudging uphill doesn't help. This is just a slog, and a grind, and something that has to be done, and something that gets done incredibly slowly.

I hope for some relief where the road turns the corner, because the road will not then be heading straight up the hillside, but angling across the slope. But when at last I get to the corner and see the gradient, I know that I have been pinning my hopes on a false horizon. There is more trouble to come, spelled out clearly in continuing steepness of a pure form.

Knowing that I am well beaten, I lay my burden down on its side on the broad grass verge, and then lay myself down beside it.

In later years my mother has told me how she herself was told the news. It was New Year's Day, 1962. The phone rang early in the morning. When she answered, the man on the other end said he was from Stoke Mandeville hospital, and asked if she was alone. She said yes, she was, apart from us two boys who were still asleep in bed. He then asked again, 'Are you sure you're alone'. And she said yes, she was. And then he told her.

I have never understood whether he was hoping there might be someone else there who would offer support to her after the news he was about to break, or hoping that my mother was alone so she wouldn't shock anyone else with her reaction to the news he was about to break. Anyway, she was alone, and he broke the news, and she had to cope alone, and grieve alone.

I don't know exactly what form of words he used, but perhaps it doesn't matter. Probably my mother knew what was coming. She is very intuitive, and bad news usually conveys itself in the manner of the person who is about to communicate it. No doubt the man from the hospital struggled to do what he had to do. It cannot have been an easy task. If his manner, across the years, appears more brusque, and less empathic, than we would expect now, then perhaps that is a mark of changing times, of development in culture from the rigidities of the fifties to current sensibilities.

Early on this New Year's Day, while the rest of the world slept on, recovering from the festivities of the night before, my mother faced a different future. And then, after a while, she knew she faced a difficult task, the first of many in these new circumstances. She had to tell her two young sons that their father was dead. How could she do that? How does any parent do that? What kind of a world produces that kind of task? She knew it had to be done, so she got hold of the two diaries, and she slid open the door to our bedroom. She stood there in the room, holding the diaries, one in each hand. She saw us lying in our bunkbeds. They were each covered by two identical colourful blankets that she had bought in setting up our home two years before. She had had her forty-second birthday six days before, and my brother would be seven years old in four weeks' time.

Flying

'Once more unto the breach, dear friends, once more, or close the wall up with our English dead...' My mother was very fond of quoting that line, amongst other Shakespeare that she'd picked up over the years. She always spoke it with relish and enjoyment. Time to move again.

My own attempts to reach the summit of this long incline, also feel like a forlorn hope in need of substantial reinforcements. When, after a serious push, the reinforcements fail to materialise, I lean my bike against a grassy bank amongst some trees overhanging the road, and perch on a convenient stone for another rest. I am embarrassingly close to the resting place I have just left, and tantalisingly close to the top; but rest it is.

In the days that followed the news that he had died, three people had quiet words with me. My Auntie Dot, amongst the strangeness, and the changes, and the different people coming and going, found a little space alone with me. She looked at me with kindness, and tiredness, and sadness, and a half smile, and said 'You're a good boy.' My Uncle Jim, a kind man, said, in his gruffer way, when he found himself alone with me, 'You're a good boy.' I felt the good intentions in their words, and accepted them, but I didn't know then what they meant, and can only guess now.

Looking back, I realise now what I couldn't know at the time, which is that although they were adults they too were grieving, and upset. They didn't really know what to do, or how to behave, or what to say. When my mum first met my dad, she was staying at Dot and Jim's house. When they got married, they got married from Dot and Jim's house. When we came to live in Leeds it was to be near them. For two years, Jim came over nearly every night and slept on our bed settee so he could help turn dad in the night. Dot would sometimes sit with dad during the day so that my mother could rush to the shops and back, or deal with something else. They'd had a strong family history with him. And now, despite all their efforts and support, he was dead, and that was how it was, and that was what had to be dealt with. When they said I was a good boy, that meant something to me. I felt more grown up when they said it. They said it to me direct, person to person - not in a group, and not mediated through my mother.

The third person to have a quiet word with me was my mother herself. She looked at me with love and sadness and a half smile, and said 'You're a good boy, aren't you.' Where before I had not known what to say when told this, by now I'd had a chance to get used to it, and think of a response. 'I try to be,' I said. I remember pondering this remarkable succession of incidents, and thinking, how strange, three different people all saying the same thing to me.

I move on from my roadside perch, and, at last, reach a point where the gradient becomes shallow enough for me to cycle again. It is such a pleasure, even though progress is still slow. It is strange how quickly a cyclist can forget he is also, in ordinary times, a walker, and begrudge the restrictions and slowness of two feet, and long for the freedom that two wheels bring.

I pedal past a car parked in a muddy lay-by on the other side of the road. Two figures inside stir and move suspiciously quickly when they detect my presence. I suspect a guilty liaison, and avert my eyes and concentrate on the purer, natural world around me. My view to the right, over a wide swathe of territory, reveals that a front of rain is approaching up the Aire valley, blotting out all before it. It does not take a meteorologist to work out that the front, and the rain, will soon be with me. I stop and quickly adorn myself in my overtrousers, whilst trying to catch and admire the weather phenomenon that is about to engulf me. There is something a little scary about the size and power of what is coming towards me, something which I can do nothing to prevent, only anticipate and experience.

The rain, when it comes, is sharp and intense, but lasts only a short while, then passes on. I pass a summit, and find myself on the other side of the hill. The sun comes out and shines on the world made fresh and clean by the passing of the rain. On my right, the roofs of the town in the valley below me glisten in the sun. A silver thread on the hills opposite reveals where a wet road is heading in just the right direction to reflect the sun's rays into my eyes.

The road I am on is downhill, but shallowly so. It stretches straight ahead of me into the distance as far as I can see, until it drops further down. I gather speed effortlessly. The wind is blowing strongly at my back, adding its weight to my progress. This is my reward for the slog up to the top. This is the kind of cycling you yearn for. This is cyclist heaven. And it goes on, and on, swooping a little through different gradients, but always downhill, always straight so I can see any traffic (of which there is very little), cruising on in a delicious, high speed, wheel-spinning, freewheeling piece of bliss.

I stand up on the pedals, staying steadily upright, not pedalling, while the wind catches the larger exposed area of my body like a sail, and pushes me along. I love the high handlebars of my new bike that let me do this in such comfort, without strain on my back. Standing like this, my awareness of my bike dims and instead focuses on the experience of effortless fast progress, with the scene shifting silently and meditatively past my eyes. It is the closest equivalent I've had to the kind of flying you can get in a dream. I have a sense of control over easy magical movement just above the surface of the earth.

The sun shines upon it all, and I realise I do not feel alone in this, but feel that my dad is around too, enjoying it with me. We would have enjoyed this together; we can enjoy it together now, because I can imagine him interested in me, looking out for me. We both exist in the same universe, where time and space may not be as they appear. Thich Nhat Hanh says there is no coming, and no going. There is no beginning and no end. Individual waves do not die, they are a part of the vast ocean of beingness. I think of my friend Leo, separated by geographical space from his son, but looking up at the sun in the sky, and saying, 'The same sun shines on my son as shines on me.' At this moment the same sun shines on me as shines on my father. We are both in the same universe, and the same universe manifests in each of us.

Swallows

The sun shines on, even as the road starts to bend, and the descent starts to steepen, and the loss of height becomes serious. I am descending into the valley again, and I have to go down doing what cyclists hate to do. I am using my brakes to slow me down. What a waste. All that slog uphill for this! I am apparently the kind of cyclist who is half way to being a good Buddhist. I am not dwelling in the past, as all memories of the good experiences only a few minutes before are quite erased. I am living in the present moment - this braking business is pure suffering – but a true Zen practitioner would transform the suffering, and enjoy the braking for its own sake.

I come to a crossroads and turn left. I am amongst houses again, but worse, I am amongst serious traffic. This is supposed to be just another little yellow road, a small vein on the blood map of the area. On the ground, at teatime, it is a surging flow of arterial dimensions, with all the motorised metallic blood cells pumping their way up and down the hill, and eyeing me, the alien in their midst, with some disfavour. As the road does its normal little routine, and starts to head uphill at the now familiar excruciating angle, I take to a conveniently adjacent pavement and disguise myself as a pedestrian. Simple-celled elements that they are, this seems to fool the vehicles, and they ignore me.

The road leaves the houses behind, but continues to climb. I continue to push and the road continues to climb. My heart beats more and more loudly, and the road continues to climb. I come to a bench at the side of the road, and immediately my posterior is magnetised to its seat. My heart pounds in a way that tells me I am not in as good a shape as I would like to be, and that I need to start moving uphill at a pace suitable for the shape I am actually in. Remember: not good shape equals slow, slow pace.

From the bench, after my own circulating blood supply assumes a pace more in keeping with that of someone destined to live longer than the next hour or so, I see swallows gathering and flying and twittering just above and around me. While the traffic struggles up and down the road in restricted convoys below them, they express life and freedom and energy. 'Off to Africa! Off to Africa!' they say. 'See you in the spring. Hope you survive the gloom of the winter. Darker days to come.'

Like most children I had a favourite colour. It had been red when my dad died. I changed it to black. I liked the occasional shock this produced. I drew a flag for my bedroom wall and coloured it in. It was the Jolly Roger, with a skull and cross bones, and a black background.

I had a lot of dilemmas. I didn't necessarily want people to know that my dad was dead, because this was very private and personal, and them knowing made me more vulnerable. I did want them to know because I needed not to feel so alone with it. It also gave me a little kudos, a little way of being special, and there wasn't much of that going around. I disliked talking about it because it meant I had to deal with other people's reactions when I was struggling to handle my own. I needed to talk about it, but with someone who was right for it, and the right person didn't seem to be around.

Going into strange shops, or meeting strange adults of any kind, was a nerve-wracking procedure. Did they know about my dad or not? If they did, would they be sensitive, or would they say something crass, that would hurt me, or confuse me? Would they ignore the fact, or be cloyingly sympathetic, or bluntly offensive? All of these ways were painful to me, because the whole situation was painful to me. There was no right way to deal with me, because everything was wrong for me.

If they didn't know about him, what then? If we had a conversation, the chances were that sooner or later the talk would come round to my dad. Then I faced an awkward dilemma – tell them he was dead, and have to deal with their reactions, or their evasions, or their questions, or their pity. Or cleverly sidestep the issue without actually lying. I wasn't that clever. It was all too difficult. I solved the dilemma by, as much as possible, avoiding those kinds of conversations, by avoiding going into strange shops, and avoiding meeting strange adults.

There was this really huge thing that had happened to me, that dominated my life, and yet I had to keep it inside me and deal with it there. Everyone around also naturally preferred it if everything was kept nice and neat on the outside. Everyone around was very helpful to me: together we kept this whole thing under wraps. We were good at it. I became skilled.

I didn't know this, but what I needed back then was a certain kind of person. Someone who knew about death and grief, because they knew themselves. Someone who was straightforward and understanding. Someone who said, 'You must be having a really hard time. If you want to talk sometime, I'd really like to listen to what it's like for you. I know I can't make it better, but I've got a couple of ideas that might be useful.' If I met someone like this I don't remember it. If someone said this to me I don't remember that either.

Brother

It's hard to leave the bench because the alternative is more struggling uphill, but despite the pleasures of the swallows, the pain of the traffic noise drives me away. At a bend a little further on, a terrace of houses affords me some diversionary interest. How do they park their cars? Those curtains are a bizarre choice. Someone's converted two houses into one. Walking back from the shops must be a trifle burdensome.

Past the terrace I lose the pavement, and am forced into the roadway, suffering further from the onslaught of noise and fumes and casual indifference. Only the frail metal of my new bike is acting as a barrier between my frailer flesh and the crunching caress of a careering car, spinning out of control through one careless flick of a driver's wrist. I would of course happily sacrifice my new bike to save my skin, but I don't somehow think it would be particularly effective. We would go down together. With this sobering assessment to spur me on, I push on up.

Near the top, I am blessed twofold. One: there is the junction where I turn on to my next road, which I know to be flat, and which I am convinced, perhaps rather optimistically, will also be almost traffic-free. Two: a rainbow appears arching across the dark clouds above me, and seems to disappear from sight at the top of the road I am on. It is impossible not to feel pleasure at so wonderful a sight, and so I do.

The slope levels out at the top, and I remount and ride again. The junction duly appears, I duly turn off, and my wishful thinking about reduced traffic turns out in fact to be a well-founded analysis. It is plateau riding again; high above the neighbouring valley, a straight road before me, the wind behind me. I make good, easy progress. The autumn day is drawing in, but my brother's house is not far, and I therefore have a safe lodging for the night.

I have made the mileage I planned. My bike has stood up to the rigours of the day and the ride. More importantly my body has stood up to them too. My bum, with the padded saddle, the flexing saddle movement, and the saddle stem suspension to aid it, remains a soreness-free zone. My legs, unused to prolonged exercise, but indulged through the day with frequent and generous rests, and a varied diet of cycling and walking (ah, all those hills), remain an ache-free zone. Even my back, which had been trying me periodically prior to the journey, and which I had feared might be an area of weakness, and might succumb to the added strain, has eased and improved slightly.

I try to work out the last time I stayed overnight with my brother. I'm sure it was when he was still single, which is a long time ago, as his eldest child Amy is now doing A levels.

Our relationship as children was the usual confused mixture. We played together very happily, from toy soldiers, to lego, to card games, to sports. For example, when we got into cricket in the back garden, we played with a certain kind of plastic ball, one that was hollow, with lots of holes in it, and therefore light and unlikely to break windows. We discovered that if you sellotaped over all the holes on one side, then you had a ball that would swing amazingly in the air when you bowled it across the garden. We spent hours doing that, and playing other games.

We also fought a lot – often acting out the wrestling we saw on the telly, but sometimes descending into real, unpleasant, angry, crying conflict.

As the older brother, I felt responsible and protective at times. And at times I even acted on this, once marching bravely into the headmistresses office at the Primary school and asking her to get his football back from the school roof where someone had kicked it, leaving him upset. At other times, I'm embarrassed to say, I was less than protective. In fact, I know sometimes I was truly horrid to him, and the fact that most older brothers are horrible to their younger siblings doesn't make it any the less unpleasant, for him then, or for me now. I squirm a little as I remember and the memory comes into conflict with the more idealised portrait of myself that I prefer to dwell on. I feel sorry for all the unkind things I did.

Another ingredient in this potent brew of fraternal stew was a smidgeon of jealousy and envy. As we grew older, particularly after we moved from Leeds when I was twelve, I always felt he had more and better friendships than I did. He would be able to go off playing with his mates, while I was stuck at home, or forced to go out on bike rides alone, and live with my fantasies of sporting glory, or the more mundane and simple desire for a friend or two that was like me.

I try and hazard a guess as to how much of my unhappiness and loneliness was standard adolescent angst, and how much of it was exacerbated by misery from unexpressed grief over the loss of my father. The answer remains indistinct, lost somewhere between the mists of time and the mysteries of my mind.

Final Address

I find my way to the house, and as I approach it I see I'm within five minutes of the estimated time of arrival I gave him a couple of days ago. I'm suitably impressed with myself, though only in a minorly obsessional way.

David greets me warmly at the door, and takes charge of me in a familiar kind of way. We lock my bike in the garage, and I bring in various bits of kit and wet clothes. He offers to wash and dry any clothes that need it, and deals with the stuff I put his way. I am used to having to fend for myself, and this is very pleasant. He makes me tea, of the fruit variety, and offers me cake and/or biscuits. He has specially bought varieties without dairy products so that I can eat them, and I am very touched that he has taken account of my awkward diet in this way. The cake, and the biscuits are also very delicious, and I celebrate my safe arrival after the testing rigours of the day by slightly overindulging myself.

I find I am experiencing my brother looking after me, and it is a very warming experience. He is very kind, and attentive, and welcoming. I guess he has learned it in our family, as our mother is a very warm and lookey-after kind of person. I wonder therefore, whether people might experience me in the same kind of way. It's an interesting insight.

Pat, my sister-in-law, and Amy, my niece, are not home yet, so my brother and I sit companionably with Johnnie, his son, who is in his mid-teens, and enjoy our little repast.

After discussing some of my adventures of the day, and some of what David has been up to lately, which includes taking up golf, and playing it with Johnnie, we fall to talking about our dad. I'm aware that David doesn't have many memories of him. He wasn't yet seven when he died.

'I remember him sitting in his wheelchair looking out of the window.' he says. 'I remember Uncle Jim coming to sleep at our house every night. Did he really do that?'

'Yes, to help turn dad in the night. I think he used to come late on in the evening, maybe mostly after we'd gone to bed. In the mornings, early, I'd see him sometimes, folding away his sheets and blankets, and then walking back home for breakfast I presume, before going to work. You know he must have done that for two years.'

'And I think he came to sleep each night after dad died as well, to look after us, because mum got that night job.'

'I'd forgotten that, but I think you're right.'

I tell him a little about how I think not going to the funeral, though standard for the time, has not been helpful to me in dealing with his death.

'Did you know you were missing it?' he asks me.

'I don't think I really knew what it was, but I think I knew I wasn't going.'

'Someone must have looked after us.'

'I've never thought of that. I don't know who it was.'

'Maybe it was Auntie Dot. She didn't seem to go out much, and she also had to look after her mother.'

'Unless we were back at school. Maybe term had started. The dates might fit.'

'And what about the body? He died in Aylesbury. They must have brought his body back to Leeds.'

All those arrangements. Someone must have had to sort them out. Someone made phone calls, and organised transport for his body, and a place for it to rest in Leeds, and a time for the funeral. And let people know, and organised tea and sandwiches afterwards.

'You know mum's been wanting to get a plaque to mark where dad's ashes are scattered,' my brother continues, 'well, I've been doing some research for her. You know, the funny thing is, I had no idea where his ashes were until eighteen months ago. I'd never asked, and never thought to wonder, somehow. Then I discovered his ashes were scattered in Leeds crematorium. When I was a student in Leeds, I went past that place every day for years and I didn't know he was there.'

'It's on my route tomorrow. I did go there once before; it was about fifteen years ago. I wanted to see what it was like. I found it quite helpful. You know, he really was dead. That kind of thing.'

It had been a grey winter's day, and I was doing my then regular weekly commute between Sheffield and home. I'd probably stopped off for therapy in Leeds, as there was a time when that was the arrangement. I'd been promising myself for a long time that I'd take the chance to go to this place that I'd never been to, and that I knew I should have gone to when I was nine. The long wait, though, had left a bit of a black hole, and I had filled it, over the years, with a dilute mix of dread and anxiety. What if it was horrible? And almost as bad, what if it was nothing, and I felt nothing?

It had been enough to give me an excuse not to make the time, when my life, as usual, seemed full enough already with work and family responsibilities. But on this day I caught the bus out there, and wandered round, under grey afternoon skies, seeing large grounds, and mature trees, and a large chapel. By this time in my life I'd been to a couple of cremation services, and had found them uninspiring. I found the crematorium uninspiring that day, and wondered what the service for my dad had been like. I didn't know, and still don't know. I don't even know who was there.

But as I left the place, through the big iron gates, and started to walk back alongside the dual carriageway, rather than wait for the bus, I found myself realising that this was the place where his physical body came to an end, and that it had really come to an end. This is where his body was burnt in the fires. And I realised this at the same time as feeling strongly again the warmth of his physical presence, and how important it had been to me. I was used to his body. I had moved it around the place in his wheelchair. I could touch him, and he was flesh, and warm, even though he mostly couldn't feel me. But with his face he could feel me, and I thought that as a child I had kissed him goodnight, and felt the rough stubble on his chin. His face and head, important parts, were still vigorously alive. And now he was gone, and his body was no more, and this was where it had happened, and I cried as I walked along the empty pavement, with playing fields on my left. But I knew a truth about his death in a way that I had not known it before, and there was relief for me in that.

'I've been there twice myself now,' says my brother.

'What was it like?'

'One time it was a beautiful day, with clear skies, and the sun shining, and it felt like a good place to be. It's quite green and wooded. And I'd found out which plot his ashes were scattered on. You don't get the exact place, but the general location.'

'I never knew that. So where is it?'

My brother roots out a piece of paper with the details on it. 'I've got a map. You can borrow it if you're going tomorrow. It's Upper Woodland Glade 1, Path 3.'

Upper Woodland Glade 1, Path 3. So that's his final address, and I always thought he was somewhere in the ether. How come I'd never done the research? I hadn't realised there would be records, and that they would be relatively simple to access. My brother had asked, and they had given him the information.

'What about the other time you went?'

'It was in February, and it was not so good. You know people put flowers and mementoes near their relatives' ashes. I think there are rules about what you can leave, but I think at Christmas some people had been leaving tinsel and other decorations, so by February it was all looking a bit sad. Too much plastic, which didn't seem to fit right among the trees and grass.'

We talk about the schools we went to in Leeds, going on the bus to Ireland Wood, and then to the new school opening at Cookridge. Later on David had gone to another new primary school that was built on land behind our bungalow. I tell him what I remember about taking a note in for Miss Rhind after dad died. He remembers several of the teachers telling him they were sorry to hear about his dad. I remember a note I found recently in mum's papers from the headmistress of the school, saying how sorry she was to hear of his death, and was there anything she could do, and it must be a comfort to have her two boys with her.

Shrine

David goes out of the room for a short while. Johnnie and I are talking about his school and other parts of his life. He is very patient with me while I ask the usual adult questions. I also tell him I'm sure his grandfather would have enjoyed meeting him, and being with him, if he had lived. I tell him also that dads are important, and that it's great to have one who takes you to things like golf that would be really hard to access on your own. Johnnie listens to me with every appearance of patience when I thus succumb to this clumsy adult dispensing of philosophy.

Pat and Amy are due back soon, and we are going to be moving more into family life mode. I head off for the bath that I have been offered, and enjoy a reviving soak, my body relishing the semi-weightless experience.

Pat has returned when I get back down, and is her usual warm and cheerful self. Given the workload that she, and all teachers, operates under, I am always a little surprised at this. An ashen-faced wreck, collapsed on the settee and unable to move seems a more reasonable kind of state to expect.

She is busy organising the tea, which we eat en famille, sitting round a table, with Amy returning from her bank cleaning job to join us part way through. Special food has been cooked to enable me to eat. I feel very included in the whole experience, and feel restored and relaxed in myself through it. It's great to be part of their everyday life, rather than meet them at the special family occasions where most of our contact now occurs.

My own family life has now essentially come to an end, at least on a day-to-day basis. After tea I phone the last member to have left. Rowan has had her first proper day at dance school in London. She is very excited about it, and about living in a flat with two other girls: 'We have so much in common, and so much to talk about.' I also phone Ewan and check he's OK, which, to my relief, he seems to be.

Fatherly jobs completed, I join the others, and we have more tea to drink, and more cake and biscuits to eat. My brother has also brought in an apple from their tree in the garden. It's a large, dark red, splendid specimen of an apple, and he slices segments off it and passes them round. It is firm and sharp and delicious, and goes well with the cake.

Family life ends here too, for the evening, as everyone heads off for a relatively early night. I am left in occupation of the living room. Not yet sleepy, I think about the crematorium, and what my brother and I had discussed. We weren't at dad's funeral. What had we missed?

I remember a couple of experiences of collective responses to death that I'd had the day before. In order to test my bike, and my systems, and my legs, I'd done a test run: a prologue, as it were, to the main trip. At eight in the morning, Mary had dropped me and my bike off at the Battery in Morecambe. There is a car park here that juts out a little into Morecambe Bay. At the end of that car park, in an obscure place, but with the magnificent bay as a backdrop, is a memorial that I'm very partial to. I'd decided it would be a suitable place to start from.

The memorial depicts in white marble a swimmer's right arm and face just above the surface of the foamy water. He wears swimming goggles. Underneath, the inscription reveals that this is a memorial to Commander Charles Gerald Forsberg, OBE, RN (Retired), who died in 2000, aged 88, and whose retirement wish was to 'sit facing Morecambe Bay and imbibe the matchless view.' 'Gerry's life embraced the sea. He was a Master Mariner, and served with courage and distinction in the Royal Navy in WW2. He was a marathon swimmer whose swims included the English Channel (world record 1957), Lough Neagh, and Loch Lomond, as well as twenty-nine crossings of this, his beloved Bay... the most gentle and amiable of men, Gerry is constantly recalled with great affection by his many friends.'

And yes, that's right – twenty-nine swims across Morecambe Bay.

On this raw Sunday morning, with grey clouds scudding by overhead, and nothing to shelter me from the fierce wind and occasional sharp rattle of rain driving in from the sea, I do not have time to ponder Gerry's remarkable exploits, or the affection of his friends, or the connections I feel whenever I see some parallels with my dad's life – the navy, the war, the sea, the being dead, the affection and respect of his friends; and some differences: commissioned rank, long swims in cold water, long life.

Instead I do as rapid a job as I can of getting my bike out of the car, and refitting the wheels that had had to come off so it would fit in there. Mary helps me reconnect the brakes, which is a two person job, then heads off while I finish packing the panniers. Anxious to get moving, away from the fierce elements, I get straight on my bike. And then I get straight off again as ominous noises emanate from the back wheel. I look, and I curse. I have managed to put the back wheel on with the chain running in a weird way round the rear derailleur. Luckily I have done no damage. I disconnect the brakes (a one person job), get the wheel off, run the chain round the correct route, and put the wheel back on. I try to connect the brakes, but fail. I try and try, but just get sore hands. I need a third hand to hold the brake arms shut and take the strain while I nudge a little cone shaped bit of metal into its correct home. My third hand has unfortunately driven off home to tea and toast.

I set off with only one brake functioning, and a voice ringing inside my head that says, 'Gerry wouldn't have put his wheel on wrong. Gerry would have made sure things were OK before he let his support go. Your dad wouldn't have put his wheel on wrong. They were practical men. They were naval men.' And then the coup de grace, 'They were real men. You're just an impostor.'

The second experience occurs a few miles inland, at Crook o' Lune, a local beauty spot, where there is Woody's tea bar and a wonderful view up the Lune valley. En route, I had paused under the shelter of a subway bridge. There I had actually managed, after careful study of the problem, and by judicious placing of my two hands in particular positions, to reconnect my back brakes by myself. It made me feel a little less of an impostor. I'd also seen some real men across the river at Halton, where some squaddies were marching along at their training camp, the NCO in front carrying his rifle at an odd angle. Later I heard them shooting, practising to kill. I could still hear them at Crook o' Lune, a couple of miles on.

I decide to stop and rest at a picnic bench overlooking the said wonderful view. I ignore the clarion call to eat meat generated by the powerful aroma of frying bacon wafting from Woody's. Near me is a kind of sculpture, depicting, in stone-cut relief, a person looking at the same view as I am looking at for real. Strange but true.

It looks like someone has been having a party by the sculpture, or an art class, as a lot of stuff is left there. I go for a closer look, and notice: a plant in a pot on the ground, a teddy bear left in the wet grass, a jug, some cards, wet, in the grass, and, attached to the sculpture, a montage of photos of someone, with a hand drawn notice that says 'We love you Tim,' and the following note:

'My dear friend Tim, I hope you know that knowing you has spoiled me forever. What we had together felt so right and I treasured our friendship. It was great being with someone who was tuned into my moods so I didn't have to explain myself. It felt so good to know that you accepted me and liked me for who I am. Just being with you, doing nothing made me happy. The friendship we had happens only once in a lifetime and I will never find another friend as loyal. Missing you so much and loving you always.'

There is also a poem, beginning, 'This awful thing has happened...' and another note that finishes: 'Although he did not die here, he loved coming here. He'd stay for breakfast and chat with his friends...This shrine helps to bring us all together again in our hearts and our minds.'

I imagine them gathering round and making their shrine, now grown a little tattered in the wind and the rain, but still conveying something of the depth of what they felt. They did it their way. I like the way they have just taken possession of this little spot and made it their own. Death can give you a peculiar authority to do what is right, and not worry about the rules.

I imagine the country full of little shrines, honouring the people who have gone, and expressing the deep collective feelings of those who are left behind. A culture that realistically recognises death embedded in the everyday structure of life.

Why should grief be restricted to cemeteries? Very regulated, very Victorian. Very dead.

News

Still not quite ready to enter the sleeping state, I idly explore the Sky options on the TV. I have never watched Sky, and I don't know how to operate the system, but I manage to flick between different channels. One of the channels announces in some words at the bottom of the screen, that the final of the Shed of the Year competition will be on in 10 minutes. I am interested in this. Ewan's mother is one of the finalists.

Her allotment shed was not entered by her, but shed-hunted by them. Spotted on a website by the programme makers in its Victorian, brick-built, decaying splendour, she was approached, and agreed to be filmed talking about it in situ. As we don't have Sky at home I had thought I would not get the chance to see her and her ancient shed on the telly. But fate has decreed otherwise. I seem to be in the right place at the right time. Or am I? I return in a few minutes to the appropriate channel, but something else seems to be on. I search around, and find another shed announcement on a different channel but still no actual shed programme.

Swallowing the disappointment of hopes thus dashed, I seek distraction in a systematic pilgrim's progress through the promised land that is TV heaven. I am amazed. I finally see the shopping channels that are the real life versions of the take-offs I have seen on ordinary, landlocked TV. There are many shopping channels. I see sports channels. I see golden oldie channels. I see news programmes. I see a programme where news is read by naked women. I see music channels. On some of these music programmes women wear less clothing than they would if they had been cycling through the Yorkshire dales today.

Harry

Leaving early I see a rainbow at the end of the road. I take this as a good sign, a symbol of harmony in my world if not the whole world. Skirting a roundabout or two, I find myself descending fast towards the bottom of the valley. The road twists and turns, and the traffic going down with me is slowed up by the bends, while I am speeded up by the hill. Our speeds are therefore relatively equal. It is not easy for a car to overtake, and I find myself in the enjoyable position for a cyclist, of cars having to wait patiently behind me for prolonged periods. Happily the drivers this morning are patient, and keep their distance. Unhappily my descent takes me past a series of beech and chestnut trees that have spilled their mast and conkers into the roadway. Here, broken and brittle and hard, they wait to upset my natural balance, threaten to upset me into the road, and leave me generally upset, mainly because I have to slow down, while the cars, with their four fat stable tyres, don't, and they swish easily past me.

The road crosses a little stone hump-backed bridge, and I turn off on to the gravelly track that is the canal tow path. At last, a genuine car-free zone. I feel a sense of profound relief to again be somewhere created on a human scale. Out of immediate danger, I can again start to take in what is around me. A neat wooden barrier stands near the side of the canal, and I cannot resist leaning my bike against it while I contemplate my surroundings. The gravel crunches under my feet, and the wind blows against my face and ruffles the surface of the canal. The canal is narrow, and the far bank, lined with trees, is only a decent long jump away. The bridge is small, and outlined in white to remind you not to bump your head. The dressed stone that form the edges of the canal and the bridge were hand cut by men and put in place by other men. The whole canal was dug by hand.

I think about my brother. As he saw me off this morning he gave me two apples. They are now safe in my saddle bag to be eaten later, but in remembering them I remember also his actions yesterday evening when he sliced an apple, and handed the slices round to his family, and to me. I suddenly see my mother doing the same action when we were children. It was a habit of hers, an intimate little custom, perhaps a reminder of times from her own childhood when apples were scarcer, and resources were shared out. He has retained the habit, and I haven't.

My brother, like myself, has grown older. We are neither of us any longer the young boys who live so vibrantly in my memory. The passing years have transmuted us, though whether into gold is a matter of debate. Nevertheless, I am interested in the aging process that brings the bones of our ancestry closer to the surface. As the years pass I detect in his face, as I detect in mine, a closer resemblance to two people. One is our mother, now in her eighties. The other is our grandfather, our father's father, Harry Armstrong.

We have a few photographs of him as an old man: for example marching with his old soldier comrades on Armistice Day parades. I never saw in him a resemblance to me: he was after all, an old man, with old man features. But as I myself, outrageously, have been increasingly affected by time, I have seen that my hair is receding at the temples in a way similar to his, and that the incised lines from my nose to the sides of my mouth are from the same mould as his. Now I see it too in my brother. It reminds me that we never saw the same thing happening with our father. He has always remained in youngish middle age.

Harry's image as a young man does exist. Among my mother's stacks of old black and white photos, I found a couple of him as a young man. One dates from about 1914, not long after he had joined up in the East Yorkshire Regiment. Freshly kitted out in his army uniform, he sits with a couple of mates, and smiles with a fresh, open face into the camera lens. A year or so later, another photo shows him as he leans against a wall, helping him maintain balance on his one remaining leg. Two other maimed men lean against the wall next to him. His face is dark, closed, with the incised lines already etched into his flesh at age thirty, instead of fifty.

Returning to work on the railways, he was given a job as a lift operator, an occupation officially reserved for disabled men.

As a child, I was unaware of any pain or tragedy in his story, unaware of the frequency with which similar stories could be told, and unaware that he was a fortunate man. His wound removed him from the conflict and therefore probably kept him alive. I may owe my own existence to that wound. My father was born in 1921.

As a child I was only aware that a grandfather with an artificial leg was an interesting piece of information to share with friends. When granddad once came to stay with us, the excitement was magnified by the arrival of a replacement artificial leg. Being aged five at the time, I thought that the best part of this phenomenon was the large cardboard box that it arrived in. My brother and I used it as a sledge to ride in down the grass bank in our back garden.

Within six months of his son's accident my grandfather was dead. He was, I think, seventy-one. Officially it was a cerebral haemorrhage. His wife, my grandmother, followed within a few more months.

Their only other child, my dad's older brother, had died a couple of years before.

Hearing the story from my mother of my grandparents' deaths, I have mostly thought of the distress to my dad, paralysed in hospital, and unable to help. I have also though of the added burden on my mother, who had to deal with solicitors and practicalities, and difficult family politics, all from many miles away.

Now, as a father with grown up sons, I think also of the pain Harry must have experienced in the suffering and loss of his two adult sons.

Imposition

Cycling along a canal towpath is a joy. It is flat and it is car-free. I also am free. I have the particular freedom of an early morning start, with the world open before me, and only my journey to pursue. I am unchallenged by phone calls or to-do lists. I simply pedal, and I move. I keep the gears low, and I therefore pedal easily, and move slowly. The elongated artificial lake alongside accompanies me silently. I steer round small pebbles, and through small puddles. I make progress through the world, and the world remains utterly indifferent. I am mobile and I am content.

I cross over the canal via a road bridge to the towpath on the other side. I enter a quiet world of green trees and leaves and bushes and me. The water in the canal is brushed by the wind, but flows nowhere. It carries no traffic. I meet no people. The world of work and hurry and noise is all around, but into this alternative world it fails to penetrate.

Three swans resting by the side of the towpath move slightly as I dismount and pass them cautiously. Just beyond them, I manoeuvre my bicycle through a metal gateway narrower at the top than at the bottom, and designed, I presume, to allow passage to buggies and wheelchairs, but not to motorbikes. Ordinary bicycles like mine can just squeeze through, but not while being ridden. Even if it is inconvenient, I am delighted that someone has put thought, and money, into infrastructure for bikes. They care! We are not totally forgotten! Not totally forgotten – praise indeed.

The sun shines, and I pass a couple of women walking along the towpath. The gloom of deep shadow engulfs me as I ride through the canyon formed by the mills at Saltaire. I am sure these mills were model working places in their day, and a big improvement on the existing industrial practice, but I still don't like their monolithic imposition on the world. The indifference of the natural world to little old me is one thing. A man-made structure that makes me feel like a worm is another.

I realise that one essential difference is permeability. With trees, and woods, and rocks, I can wander in and around and through them, and our relative separateness is a natural part of the deal. It is possible for buildings to be built and designed that also convey something of the same, organic, message. On both sides of me now, however, long walls, built with care and architectural input, high enough to include series of windows well above my head, and broken up by chimneys and different levels, convey a clear message: 'no way in, no way through'. Somewhere, no doubt, there is an entrance, through which workers used to pour, and remain amongst the clattering machinery till their day's work was done, remain till their life's work was done.

I look back, and the two women are dots in the distance. Their ancestors probably worked in these mills. If I had lived here a hundred years ago I might have counted myself lucky to do the same.

Instead I feel even more fortunate to be free, to be exploring, to be journeying. Beyond the mills, the sun continues to smile, and I continue.

Grief

I come to a set of locks. I love locks. They enable people to raise big boats up through significant vertical heights. They do it without mechanical power. They do it through an elegantly simple system that harnesses the force of gravity. They are powerful tools but can be operated by almost anybody, even me. They just sit there waiting until they are needed.

These ones are stone-built, big, deep. Sturdy white-painted barriers surround the parts where a vertiginous person like me might be tempted to fall in. Neat stone staircases and little wooden bridges enable access to the parts that canal boat people need to reach. There are bollards to tie your boat to, and iron ladders to take you up and down the sides and into the depths.

From below, the massive wooden lock gates tower up to the big beams at the top. When the level of water is equal on each side, you use the big beams to swing the gates open. When the water levels are unequal, as they are at the moment, then the weight of water against the far side serves to force the gates shut, exerting pressure on their slight V shape in a similar way, though in a different plane, to the forces on a hump-backed bridge.

The weight of water against these particular gates does force them shut, but it is not a perfect operation. Time's deterioration, and a less than thorough maintenance programme, have created a wonderful spectacle. From various gaps in the gates, jets of water are arcing and spurting across the deep entranceway to the lock. Glittering in the sunshine, they create their own water feature, a random criss-crossing of fountainous liquid gushing under pressure from the reservoir behind.

I stand and admire them, their limpid tracery well set-off by the green ferns growing profusely on the walls and gates. The ferns grow at the margin where the dry area meets the areas soaked when the sluice gates are raised to let out the water behind.

As I look more closely I see that in two or three places more water is emerging, not from the gates, but from gaps between the stones themselves, having found a mysterious underground route from the lock.

I think of dammed-up grief, and the powerful way in which it will force an outlet if it can, spurting out in unexpected places. Sometimes the spurting out happens in weird ways; sometimes, as here, the result can be beautiful. But grief held back without release risks turning sour and becoming poison.

This was the lesson I learned in my experience of therapy, where I worked hard to widen those little channels of escape that my grief had managed to create, and to loosen the bonds of convention that had contributed to the constriction in the first place.

I wander across the little footbridge to the other side of the lock complex. Here, hidden from the towpath side, a little channel has been created to take the run-off from the upper levels of the lock system. A couple of yards wide, flat bottomed with stone, hung over with trees, it runs smoothly down at a regular angle. The water in it chatters evenly down the incline without fuss or ferment.

I think of grief again. If it's allowed its course, grief just flows, in the end, like this. It's part of the flow of life, flowing on. It is energy, which needs to move; and when it's allowed to move then it can transform, as all energy can, into something light and fantastic.

Bounty

I roll on down the path. It is autumn, and mellow fruits adorn my passage, and, in places, prolifically scattered beneath their producer tree, succumb beneath my wheels. In thinking about this journey, I had wondered how many dead animals I would pass at the side of the road, and whether I should keep a tally of species and numbers: a road-kill progress across England. But I had not anticipated this natural, gentler, and more satisfying bounty. Crab apples, beech mast, conkers, alder cones, and hazel nuts grace my passage. Berries - beautiful displays of dark purple elder, tempting black brambles, less tempting red and green brambles, long strings of bright red ones whose name I don't know - are everywhere apparent, sometimes crowding in on me from the side to narrow my path. And everywhere too the musty smell of dank autumn processes speaks of the fine line between fruition and decay.

I come across another set of locks, stop to admire them, and regret their gates are close fitting enough to prevent any repeat of water magic. Above, in a blue sky with minimal clouds, another rainbow arcs across, my second of the day.

I come to a point where the river reappears from over on my left, and flows along just below me at the bottom of a steep, wooded slope so that the towpath is a narrow strip of land between the canal on one side and the river on the other. I pause and rest.

There are canal boats tied up on the other bank, double-banked in places. They are probably set for the winter, as they all look closed off and uninhabited. Their names – Bobbies Girl, Maranjee, Paris, India, Blue Heron – and their homely appearance seem very sweet, and I am filled with a powerful longing to live on one for a time. I want to experience the snail's freedom of wandering with a home, and stopping any place I choose. It would be so fantastic. My fantasies take me over completely and run off with me. This is not a difficult thing to do, susceptible as I am to escapist dreaming.

I reach into my pannier and take out one of the apples my brother gave me, cut it in half, and eat one of the halves. It is another fruit of autumn, taken from the tree in his garden: beautiful dark red skin, and firm, sharp, sweet flesh. Also in my pannier are some of the special biscuits, which he has wrapped in foil. As I unwrap the foil to eat one, I feel very touched by his care, and thoughtfulness. I feel looked after by him, and it is a strange, unusual feeling that leaves me tearful. Oh God, I say to myself, as I feel the energy rise in my throat, and the prickling around my eyes, surely I'm not crying again, am I? But I am, and I must let it happen, and it does happen, and then passes away after a while.

In the aftermath, I think of my brother with affection, and then start to worry about what happened between us as children. Someday, I think, maybe I could say sorry to him for the times when I was unkind to him, or said unkind things. I tried, as an older brother, to behave responsibly to him, and feel I succeeded at times. But at other times the strain was too great, and the temptation to use my greater age and power to hurt or wound was too much, and I succumbed. Now I feel guilty, and rather stuck in the guilt. I'm sorry, I say to him in my mind, I'm sorry for any unkindness, then or since.

Killed

As I move on again, another rainbow appears against a clear blue sky, its end arcing diagonally down into the horizon. It's my third of the day, and it's still quite early. It could be a record breaker of a rainbow day. A callow voice inside starts pontificating on the normal association of rainbows with rain and cloud, and the unusual number I have seen against a clear sky, but I ignore it, and it goes away. I prefer to appreciate how wonderful it is, and to add to my pleasure by counting.

My wonder in a natural phenomenon that must have amazed people back at the start of proto human prehistory is interrupted by a wonder of the modern era. My mobile beeps to alert me to a text. Mary is assuming that I am on my way and that all is well. I reply that the sun is beautiful, and that all is, indeed, well.

Beauty, nature, and humans (plus death) come together in a different configuration a few yards further on. A large, handwritten notice headed 'KILLED' continues: 'A youth armed with a bow and arrow has shot and left swans to die. The police and the RSPCA are aware. Anyone with information should call the police.'

I have always found swans a little scary, as well as beautiful, because of their size and potential fierceness. Now, as well as swans, I can be afraid of a homicidal youth with a bow and arrow, and an anonymous but vengeful bird lover turned copper's nark.

The river heads off to wander further afield, and is replaced by the railway, which cuddles up to the canal for a while.

A canal boat from Selby, towards which I am heading, passes me at the usual slow, sensible speed, followed by another canal boat at a similar slow sensible speed. We exchange 'Good mornings'.

My own speed is also slow and sensible. The surface of the towpath continues to vary between stony and smooth, and my attention must vary between the surface and the surroundings. In one place cyclists previous to me, in search, like all cyclists, of the best route, have shifted from the stony path to the grass verge alongside. Here continual use has worn away some of the grass and created a smooth, beaten earth cycleway close to the canal.

The width of this cycleway is about six inches. You see, we cyclists are an abstemious lot. Our efficient means of transport, (the most efficient in the history of the world; well, maybe except for sailing boats), needs the most minimal of support systems. We don't ask for motorways, we don't even need roadways. All we need are thin strips of tarmac about six inches wide, criss-crossing the whole country. Then we'd be happy.

I am still happy even just with a stony towpath. The canal-side experience, as the sun shines down, and peace reigns, is deeply pleasurable.

Ahead of me, a low swing bridge is in place across the canal. From the field on one side to the field on the other a whole herd of Friesians is shuffling and snorting and shoving their way across. Various of their number pause to stare at me, and then get bumped into motion again by their less curious cousins behind. I know my place in the grand bucolic scheme of things, and wait them out.

I examine the map. There is a place ahead where I had been planning to leave the canal. If I leave at the junction after that instead, I can extend my canal stay by a mile and a half, and still retain the integrity of my original route. Satisfied with the extra pleasure I have granted myself, and the path before me now being open and herdless, I cycle on into the blue yonder.

Lou and me

Lou Read joins me on my journey. In relaxed mode, I cycle along the towpath, with the sunshine blessing the day, and the words of 'Satellite of Love' reverberating through my skull. Or rather, the words that I know. This turns out to be three actual words, plus one proto word repeated three times: 'doo doo doo satellite of love, doo doo doo satellite of love, doo doo doo satellite of love, sat-e-llite of love.' Nothing daunted, I sing along with Lou anyway and we have a great time together. In my world, Lou is very laid back about his songs.

I pause at a bench to admire the last of the green fields around me, for the city is starting to close in. I eat another of the biscuits wrapped in foil, a small package of love. I realise that in this contact with my brother I am getting some clues as to how our father might have been if he had lived to grow older. I feel again the tension in my nine year old body, the longing for loving contact from the man I loved. There has been an absence there ever since, and the gentle, parental care of my brother has reminded me of the gap.

I know from my work with men over the years that it doesn't take death to create an emotionally barren relationship between father and son. Too many men I have known have experienced their living fathers as distant, emotionally absent figures. It's the culture we live in. There are broadly three choices for these men with absent fathers: to cut off emotionally themselves and repeat the pattern with their sons; to get angry and blame their fathers; or to grieve, and try to understand how it happened, and seek to make connections. The last is the hardest to do.

In the experiences of these men, I have seen that it is the lack of love that creates grief, not the lack of the person. If he had lived, my own father may have become cut off himself as he grew older. It's common enough in our culture. The strength of my longing for his love may also, I know, have developed a fantasy for me about who he was, and what he was capable of. I can never check that out. Men whose fathers are still alive, even if emotionally absent, can still go and see them. They may get clues as to the nature of their history, and they can live in hope of a redemption. Transformations can occur. Energy sometimes moves in mysterious ways.

I realise I must have been a difficult child to try and help. I recall the tension in me around the fear of betraying him. I longed for my father, but when other men – my uncles, say – offered substitute affection and help, I was in a terrible dilemma. They were the wrong man. If I accepted too much from them it would be a betrayal of my father. I might start to forget him. He might be upset, in heaven, looking down. He might turn up again one day, cured, as I hoped, and where would I be then? I had to tread a thin line between getting the affection I needed and honouring his primacy in my life.

At times I probably seemed awkward, or prickly, or distant. When adolescence came along, I was already perfectly prepared for the role.

Forklift toilet

The time comes to leave the canal. I am reluctant in the extreme. The way is flat, and peaceful, and now grown familiar to me. I like the bushes, and the black elderberries hanging juicily down, and the varied musty smells of autumn decay assailing my nostrils as I pass along the towpath. There is more canal ahead that I may never see. I will re-join it later in the day further on, but what about the bit in the middle? Will I ever know what delights I might be missing? The canal disappears mysteriously and temptingly round a bend while I go off on to a minor road that crosses the canal by a small hump-backed bridge.

As if to reassure me that the change in environment is indeed the right decision, a rainbow appears. It hangs in a blue sky dotted with occasional clouds, a harbinger of harmony enhancing the stone houses and gardened slopes of the city beneath.

I am on the outskirts of Leeds, and I make my way warily through suburbia ancient and modern. I cross the river on a bridge now denied to cars, and feel the welcome glow of superior contentment. I edge carefully across a main road and seek refuge in a residential street with woods on one side and large houses with mature gardens on the other, and no people to be seen.

I pause at the other end of this street before venturing again into the busyness of the road system. I am approaching my childhood home, and I want to get my bearings, both inner and outer, before heading any further.

I am diverted from my considerations, and entertained, by a forklift truck which appears out of a nearby drive and proceeds slowly along the road carrying a mobile toilet. It trails a length of hazard tape which eventually drops off and lies in the road. The forklift truck, and the toilet, disappear into another driveway.

My map tells me that I am in Horsforth, and that soon I will be in Cookridge, which is where we were living when my dad died. A mile down the road I can expect to start recognising places.

My inner guidebook tells me that there is no compulsion to do anything I don't want to. In planning the journey I had thought to write to whoever lives now in our bungalow, and ask if I might visit. I hadn't written: it all seemed too complicated to explain, and it would have tied me to a timetable. I preferred to leave it to chance. I remind myself now that I don't have to stop, or knock on the door, or make contact of any kind. If I want to knock I will, if I don't I won't. Whatever I feel is OK. My plan is vague: just to wander around Cookridge a bit. Whatever happens is cool.

If I need to reassure myself this much, I know I must be feeling nervous. What will I remember? What would I prefer to have left forgotten? Will it all be anticlimactic or bathetic?

I launch myself and my bike back into the turbulent flow of traffic. I negotiate a serious roundabout and head off up a road marked in yellow on the map, which should indicate a minor road. But here in the city even minor roads can have major traffic, and this is one of them. It's also uphill, and before long I am walking on the pavement. Walking and pushing.

I glance around curiously in case I get a flash of recognition, but all remains quiet on the internal memory front. Mostly what I see is cars, which is a phenomenon that must have increased extraordinarily since I was a child here in the early sixties. If the cars are not driving along the road by me, then they are parked by me, and indeed, parked by everything and everyone. Parked cars litter the road, and the verges, and any space that isn't being used for something else. As I reach the top of the hill and see the road swoop down and up ahead of me, what mainly hits my attention is the sun glinting on the multi coloured array of metallic roofs.

I come to Horsforth. I pass the station. I know I have got off trains at this station as a child, but there is no glimmer of recognition.

I head up the hill closer to home territory, past the Fox and Hounds pub, which again, I do not remember. I do not have a feel for anything. I do not have a feel for my eight year old former being, for whom these streets were home turf. The roads are now all so trafficky. They are dirty, and stinking, and noisy, and dangerous. I cannot believe that I cycled all around here from age eight onwards. It would be lethal for a child now. Back then it was a safer time – from traffic if not from predators.

I pass a little row of shops. I want to remember the times when I passed them as a child, when they would have been a marker in my world, and I would have known what each sold. But nothing comes back.

What I do remember is a homework task for geography. We were told to map the streets round our home, which meant me going out into the dark winter's night and drawing little diagrams with cold hands by the light of the street lamps. Even in the autumn daylight now, the strangeness and fear of that experience comes back. My fear was not of the dark or the cold, but of the anger of the teacher if I failed to do it correctly.

A residential street, the first to appear on my left since I started up this hill from the station catches my attention. It contours levelly along the hillside, its fifties bungalows and semis looking innocuous and unexceptional. I've got a feeling that I know this street, and that there is a little ginnel at the end which takes you through to the beck and the woods where we used to play. I swing my bike along the road to check it out.

If I'm right then I have reached a place of memory. The memory is this: a small group of us had got into conflict with another group of boys from school, and we had ended up running away from them. There were more of them than there were of us, and they were also tougher than us. It was not a serious conflict. There was some fear for us, but also a little excitement in the chase. We had run from the woods through the ginnel and into the street, and then slowed down. We felt safer in sight of people's houses, and also only one other boy was bothering to chase us by this time. I could remember his name: it was David Hicks. We ended the episode with some ritual name calling from a safe distance, and he turned back. I have often thought since that we missed a trick. He was alone and therefore outnumbered by us. We should have turned back towards him and made him run from us. That would have saved more face. But we didn't; we were not well versed in the techniques of intimidation in those days.

As I reach the end of the street, I see that there is a turning circle for cars. Between two of the gardens, there is a ginnel. A small barrier discourages bikes, but I manoeuvre mine past, and make my way between garden fences towards the dark of the woods behind.

This is the place I ran through over forty years ago. I am amazed it is still here. But it is, and I am back on home territory.

Rock Shelter

In the shade of the woods, holding my bike upright on the earthen path, I am still not really sure this is a place I know. The immediate surroundings hold no certainty for me. I know my memories of childhood places will be selective, and patchy, as almost all memories are. Some parts missing altogether, other parts sharp and clear, some bits vague and misty. I realise I have a vague and misty sense of a bridge over the railway, and that we used to cross it to get to a pond on the other side. One time the pond was frozen. I head down a path, and in a few yards I can see a footbridge. Well, I think to myself, the evidence is getting pretty strong here.

Leaving my bike leaning against a tree, I run up the steps and look down on the other, unwooded side of the railway. That could be the remains of a filled in pond there. The evidence is inconclusive, but I'm starting to feel excited. I know this is the place.

Back over the bridge, I collect my bike and walk further back up the path. There is the beck. It must be the one. Memories of classic small boy adventures come flooding back: fishing for tiddlers with nets, taking them home in jam jars and then finding them dead the next day; damming the beck; seeing water rats; inventing dares for people to do. Forty years on it looks a pale, puny reflection of the exciting watercourse of my childhood.

Nevertheless, I'm delighted to find it again. I progress along the path past humps and bumps that make it clear that local children with bikes still make good use of the place for play. Towards the edge – it's a very small wood really – I can see blue sky ahead through the last few trees. On my right there is a rock feature that I take to be the remnants of ancient small-scale local quarrying. Adorned with a little bit of tired graffiti, it forms a rough rock face which is at most nine or ten feet high. Then in one of those extraordinary transformations of perception that leaves me laughing out loud it becomes - the rock shelter.

The rock shelter! Now I know for certain this is my place. I walk along the line of rock until I reach a point where there is a slight overhang, then I stand with my back to the rock. I look out over the quiet wooded dell, with the sunshine coming in patches through the leaves above to illuminate grasses and flowers and broken branches on the ground. There is no one about.

There was no-one about when I stood here forty years ago, sheltering from the rain. It had started while we were out playing, my friends and I. They had rushed off home. I had remained, and I was joined by another boy. I didn't really know him very well, but he was friendly enough, and while the rain dripped down in front of us we had a conversation. He knew more about me than I knew about him, because he turned to me with a strange smile and said, 'Looks like we're in the same boat now, Pete.' He used that expression: 'in the same boat,' and he knew my name. He continued, 'my dad's just died, too.'

It was a moment of sharing. I had found someone who was like me. I felt adult – I was having a real conversation about real things that mattered to me. This boy must know some at least of what I was feeling. We stood a long time at the rock shelter, talking and watching the rain. When at last the rain cleared, I was excited about what had happened, and wanted to do something with it. I didn't particularly know what to do, but maybe that's a part of growing up.

Strangely I do not recall any contact with the boy again. I don't remember his name, and am not sure I ever knew it. He didn't go to the same school. I don't think he was part of our usual network of friends.

I may also have been put off by what happened when I got home. Still excited, I tried to tell my mother about the rock shelter, and the boy, and the important sharing. But she'd been worried by how long I'd been out, and was a bit cross as a result. She wasn't in the mood for confidences, and the moment faded in the air between us, and was never revived.

Field fight

A few yards beyond the rock shelter is the edge of the woods, and beyond the edge of the woods is the field, and it's still there. I'm surprised. After forty years I had really expected it to be built over. All around its distant rim is visible the red rust of the large housing estate built in the fifties and sixties. But the housing has encroached no further. The beck still winds down the left hand side of the field. The trees mark out where the beck runs. The farm at the top of the little hill near the entrance to the railway tunnel is still there.

What is different is that the farmer has made a determined effort to repel visitors. Where once we passed freely between field and woods, there are now several fierce strands of barbed wire, as if to say 'we'd really be rather grateful if you could consider playing elsewhere.' Or some such.

The field looks unplayed in. It is covered in long dried, yellow grass. In my memory it was green, and we played in it a lot.

It was where a group of us decided to have a stone throwing fight, and as our team ran up the hill to take up our positions, my best friend Charles was hit on the back. We thought they'd started throwing stones early and he turned to shout, 'Yaagh, didn't hurt anyway.' But it was not a stone they'd thrown, but the sheath knife I'd dropped, and which someone had tried to return by throwing. It had hit Charles handle first.

It was where we met some older boys who'd set themselves initiation tests for their gang. Like dangling from the high branches of certain fallen trees and then dropping to the ground. Philip Morris's older brother was one of them. These boys seemed like men to us and seemed to have reached a size and toughness that was beyond our ken.

And this was where I had the fight with Philip Morris, who before this was my friend, and after it too.

It happens like this: I am with my younger brother, and we bump into Philip, who is with two or three older boys. I don't like them, and presumably they don't like me. Because somehow the encounter degenerates into them picking on me, and making fun of me. They bump into me from each side, as though it is a rough dance, and they find this funny. They know I don't find it funny. They know what they are doing. I can't, or won't, get away. I feel stubborn. I am also frightened, with a sick feeling in my stomach. I can't understand why they are doing this, or why Philip is letting them. They are his friends.

The boys decide it's a good idea if Philip and I fight each other. They make us do it. I don't want to, but he doesn't say no, and he is there with his small pug face trying to hurt me, so I fight back. I am near tears from the upset, and the strong feelings of it all. There must have been breaks in what probably amounted to pushing and shoving and wrestling, because at one point I did something I'd never done before: I told my brother to go home and get help, get mum. And he went running off across the field and they let him go. Probably they would have let me go too, if I had run, but I didn't.

So we fight some more, and they laugh some more, and it feels more and more like a nightmare. Philip and I stand facing each other. He is breathing heavily and he is upset. He is near tears. Perhaps, I imagine, he had thought he could beat me, and gain some kudos with his lousy older mates. And now it's not working out like that. In his upset, his lip curls and he sticks his jaw out at me and points to it saying, 'Hit me. Go on then, hit me.' And I am angry and upset enough to do it. Like in the films I've watched. And I am surprised that I hit him with my fist because I've never hit anyone like that before. And he is surprised also, because I do hit him, and I hurt him, and the shock is in his eyes, followed by his tears.

And away across the field I see three figures walking over. I recognise them as my mother and my uncle Jim, and my brother, and I know that help is at hand, and if I can survive a few minutes more then it will all be over.

One of the boys notices them too.

'Look, his mum and dad are coming,' he says.

'No, it can't be,' says another, 'his dad's dead.'

And he says it with such carelessness, with such a tinge of amusement and cleverness, that I am enraged and lash out all around. I hardly know him, I don't like him, but he knows about my dad.

Salvation comes, and my mother and Uncle Jim arrive, walking steadily up. They restore order and normality to the world. They speak seriously to the boys and tell them that if two boys have a fight then it's not fair to join in and gang up on one of them. They take me home.

At school on Monday, I tell Philip that I hadn't wanted to fight him. 'I didn't want to fight you either,' he says.

Church

I realise this is my territory. This is the turf over which I roamed and played and fought and cried and laughed. I feel that I belonged here, and that here belonged to me. The realisation is the stranger for being unexpected. I hadn't looked to feel a sense of belonging, a sense of ownership. I'd forgotten that it's possible to feel like that. I don't feel like that, as an adult, about where I live now. I don't feel like that, as an adult, about this place now. But as a child, this was my world, and I belonged here, and I wandered through it, making it mine.

I am about to turn from the barbed wire, and the field, and my memories, when another rainbow appears, faintly. This time the background is grey cloud, low on the horizon. The rainbow's end drops into the ground just by the side of the farm on the hill. I think it might be my fifth rainbow of the day, but I'm not keeping a strict count. I'm concerned about this. Perhaps overexposure to rainbows will tinge me with ethereality. Will I lose my capacity to count accurately, and obsessively?

Regaining the road, I cycle back a little, and then on up the hill. I take another left turn, and pass by more fifties and sixties houses. Many of them have undergone makeovers, with extensions, or conservatories, or paved front gardens. People are absent, but as with any residential area, no doubt the busyness returns at certain times of the day and week.

I am effectively skirting the edge of the field, so that the houses on my left back on to it. My memory says there is another way through them on to the field, and my memory is right. A little passage between the houses is still there, though the field itself is blocked off. I cycle on. Where next?

The central point in all this is our bungalow, the one we had had built so dad could come home and live in it with us. It looms a little in my awareness, and I decide to approach it circumspectly, to leave it till a little later.

I have seen it once since I was a child. About fifteen years before, when the kids were little, we were driving through Leeds, and I made a detour so we could go past it, and I could show them where I had lived. We had paused the car, and gazed a little. It was an ordinary bungalow, made of bricks and mortar. It looked very ordinary. We drove on.

The advantage of being on a bike now is that I am part of what is around me, not separated from it by glass and metal. And I am moving at a pace that lets me make connections between the land and my mind that can only be done at a human pace. I can stop and examine things more closely, or explore an interesting side show.

I do in fact go down a very short side road that I pass, even though I lose height and will have to regain it on the way back. At the bottom is the field, fenced off. But clearly this road was built so that the estate could be expanded on to the field in the future. I feel delighted that development has so far been repulsed. One hearty cheer for the planners and the politicians.

I am surprised to find I still have a general sense of the layout of the estate. However the details are gone, so I keep getting little surprises where my vague intuitions are confounded by a different, sharper reality.

I want to find my way to the shops at the corner of the road near our house. There was a newsagent there where I got my comics from, and also got an encyclopaedia in weekly parts called 'Knowledge.' I never finished collecting it before my interest in 'Knowledge' knowledge waned.

But I seem to have missed the right turn, because I find myself pushing my bike up an endlessly long road of houses with driveways, and panel fences, and leylandii, and grass verges between the pavement and the road. I stay relaxed about it. I'm not in any hurry to get somewhere in amongst all this. I've been imagining this return for a long time. I'm happy to savour the moments, whatever they are.

At the top of the road, I come to the end of the estate, and the start of some older houses, together with the signs of a bus route. Where I thought I would be, wouldn't be like this, so amidst mental confusion, I work out from the map where I actually am, and allow the slightly painful readjustment in my head to take place. I'm actually quite a long way out from the bungalow, and need to work my way back.

On the way I come to the church, and pause to look. It's a modern church, built of brick, with a brick tower in the middle and the pattern of a cross picked out in darker bricks on the near wall. A wooden cross stands in the garden amongst trees.

This is somewhere that figures powerfully in my memories. It was the place where I was sent for Sunday school, but instead of Christian charity, I learned what it is like to be mercilessly teased by older boys. I was made to feel bad and weak for being who I was. I grew to hate the place, and the boys, and the vicar who failed to notice what was happening or do anything about it.

The memories are powerful, but they are composed mainly of feelings – pain, and shame, and humiliation, and powerlessness – together with a visual sense of malevolent boys' leers, the claustrophobic pews where we sat, and the ineffectual indifference of the vicar as he wandered off at frequent intervals to his little back room, so enabling my tormentors to continue their vicious little hobby.

The memories do not include the outside of this ordinary brick building. I know it is the right place, because I remember the location well. I am slightly surprised that it is still here and that I feel so little sense of connection with it given its place in my internal history.

As I stand looking, a man approaches the church and we exchange polite greetings. I wonder if he is the current vicar, and consider fleetingly whether I should engage him in conversation about the shortcomings of one of his predecessors. But it doesn't seem right, and the moment passes.

As I turn away I also wonder why I did not extricate myself from the situation all those years ago. My adult self imagines creating a fuss, or complaining to the vicar, or starting a fight with one of the boys, or telling my mother. I did none of these things, only confided my misery to my diary, and resolved there not to let any of my hurt feelings show, because that only made it worse. As a child, less familiar with what constitutes 'normal' or unacceptable, we rely more on others to help us decide what is bearable and what is unbearable.

My brother saved me in the end by reading my diary and telling my mother, who then stopped sending me. I cannot recall whether the fight in the field came after the Sunday school. I hope so, as that would at least show a development in my capacity to ask for help.

Opposite the church is a small community hall. Again, I recall the location, and associated memories of waiting here for the start of a May procession with floats and a May Queen, but of the building itself, nothing. Now it is being used as the venue for a toddler group, and mums and small children are emerging. Their squawks and excited cries are a reminder of the immediacy of life as a child.

Up from the hall is the street my best friend Charles used to live on. I go up it to see if I can identify his house. He lived a couple of notches up the social scale from us, in a big older semi, with a very lengthy back garden where we happily constructed the most enormously complex den with many rooms and elaborate entrance passageways. I know the rough location, but the houses have all been made over (we're still a couple of notches up the social scale here), and the paved, landscaped front gardens and remodelled fronts contribute to the further confusion of my mind.

At the top of his street I see the Methodist church where I went to cubs (Charles and some of my other friends went there, so I joined them) and then nervously, I turn back, and head down the hill towards the focus of this morning. I see the house on the corner where Auntie Dot and Uncle Jim lived. This is getting closer. I remember parties there and the great treasure hunts that Uncle Jim made up for us, and the teas that Auntie Dot prepared. I see the school that was built in the woods behind our bungalow, where my brother went but not I. I see the shops that were built on the corner after we moved here. I see the bus stop where I waited to catch the bus to my secondary school when the time came to leave primary. I turn off right on to my old street, and there it is. I have arrived.

Here

It is still an ordinary looking bungalow, made of bricks and mortar, but in the years since I lived in it, and in the years since I saw it last, it too has changed. Gone are the open lawns at the front, with the path through the middle up to the front door. Instead, a hedge surrounds a paved front area in the modern style. As I pause and look, standing with my bike, I see that there is a man in the far corner, working on some repairs to the fence. As if in a dream, I find myself walking across the paving towards him. This is how it has been in my imaginings of this moment. No need to knock, and be frightened. No need to quietly leave and feel pusillanimous.

'Hello,' I call.

He turns to face me. He doesn't seem phased.

'Can I ask, do you live here?' I ask (he might be a handyman, or builder.)

'Yes, I do' he says, evenly. I have reached him by this time. I sense him appraising me, but he still seems relaxed, and open. He's a man several years older than myself, I would guess.

I pause very briefly, unsure what to say. There's a lot to explain, and my fantasies never provided any details for this part. 'I used to live here, as a child,' I say, 'when it was first built. I'm on a cycling trip, and was passing. I haven't been here for many years.'

'Ah,' he says. He's interested. He looks at me slightly quizzically. 'It was a disabled house wasn't it? I know someone who used to live next door. They've told me about it.'

Now this I hadn't expected at all. My fantasies had someone living here who knew nothing at all about its history. I was going to have to tell them. This man, this stranger, already knows about my dad.

'Yes, that was my dad. He was badly hurt in an accident, and left paralysed. We had this place built so he could live here at home with us.'

'He was in the services, wasn't he? In the RAF.' He sounds a bit tentative here. 'That's what I was told.'

This is another shock. He knows more information about my father. The broad area is correct even if the detail is not. How does he know, or rather, who does he know, after all this time, who knows about my dad?

'He was in the navy,' I say. 'He was a PTI.' The man is listening carefully. He's interested, I can tell, and not just being polite. It's easy to continue a little. 'We moved in here just before Christmas 1959. There were still builders around, finishing off bits and pieces. I remember my mother telling me how she was trying to wash the kitchen floor, while they came in and out in their boots. I was seven at the time, and we lived here till I was twelve, and then moved away.'

How much to say, and when. That's always been my dilemma. How much do I try and protect the other person from the painful truth, and how much do I try and protect myself from their reaction. This man seems solid, so I continue.

'He died a couple of years after we moved in.'

I usually feel a bit better when that difficult bit of information is out in the open. There's less room for misunderstanding now, less need to worry about accidental crossings of social conventions, less risk of general embarrassment.

'He went away for a check-up in the hospital, and died there.'

That's to reassure him that my dad didn't die actually in the house. Some people feel peculiar about that kind of thing. I doubt this man would, but now he doesn't have to wonder.

I live now in a house which people have inhabited for over three hundred years. I realised a while back that lots of the inhabitants would have died in the house, hospitals during most of that period not being very commonplace as dying places. I was strangely pleased when I realised this.

'So how do you know the history of the house?' I ask.

'I know the Berrisfords from church,' he says. 'Mrs Berrisford lived next door. She's told me lots of stories from that time. She still lives round here – not far away.'

The name doesn't ring any bells, and I'm confused, but I don't want to put a block on things. I ought to know these people. Maybe there's something I've forgotten from those days.

'The people I remember from that time living next door were called Peel, I think.' I'm sure they were called Peel, but there's no need to get into an argument here. Let's keep this conversation going.

'He was a bank manager, for the Midland I think. They had two girls, one older than me, and one older than my brother.' I'm spraying out information trying to resolve the mystery, but it remains unsolved, and we pass on to other subjects.

We chat quite warmly. He tells me something of his past.

'I was in the army for twelve years. Came out in 1975.'

Ah, that explains his interest in, and familiarity with, service matters.

'I've lived around this area ever since. My children have grown up here, and now we have grandchildren. They go to the school at the back here.'

'My brother went there for a short while when it was first built, though I never did. I remember before it was built there were just birch woods there. We used to play in them a lot. They were just over the back garden fence.'

I'm finding it incredibly exciting to converse with someone about my childhood, and find that they have various reference points where our knowledge coincides. I can tell people that my brother went to a school at the back of our house, but if they don't know the place, then it's like talking into a vacuum. When I tell this man, there's a solid response, and it makes me feel more solid too. Memory is very powerful, but then so are dreams and fantasies. After years of just memories, a little tinge of doubt starts to creep in. This morning, here on this paved area, holding my bike upright, I'm getting confirmation that I wasn't just imagining all that stuff. It really happened.

He looks at me, and asks tentatively, 'Would you like to look round?'

'I'd love to,' I say.

We wheel my bike through a gate at the side of the house.

'I'm doing a cycle trip across England over a few days,' I say. 'I'm passing through various places that were or are personally important to me. I'm grateful for the chance to see this place again. It's always had such a big place in my memories. Have you lived here long yourself?'

'About four years. Though I've had my eye on it for a long time. It's the only bungalow on a double plot in the whole area. When it came on the market I was very keen to get it.'

I lock up my bike by the side of the house and leave it. I look around.

'Where this new shed is, is where I used to have a vegetable garden. My uncle Jim, who lived nearby, used to help me do it.'

'I put that shed in myself recently.'

Just behind the shed I spot something else, which I get excited about.

'That little wall there, I remember that.' It's a low wall, maybe a foot high, which acts as the boundary of a terrace, holding back the soil in the other part of the garden where it goes up a level. 'I used to practice long jumps off it. I'd run from over there and land in the loose soil here.' And then measure it of course, and record it. And deduct the height of the wall from the length of the jump to try and be fair, even though I knew the high take-off would give me an advantage greater than that. I was cheating myself, but at least I knew it.

We look now at the rest of the garden. I fail to recognise anything more than the little wall. Gone, long gone probably, are the fence at the back, the birch hedge I tried to cultivate, the grass that I remember. Instead there is a mature suburban garden. We go past the new conservatory that was not even dreamt of in my day. We go past the kitchen window and the garage.

'I remember the garage. That flat roof was great for climbing on. And we used to tie hankies to plastic soldiers as parachutes, and then throw them off from there into the garden.'

My host shows me, hidden amongst shrubs, a gate in the fence to the neighbouring house. 'This is the gate Mrs Berrisford told me about. It was put in when she was a child so that everyone could get through to the other's garden without going round. I've left it in, though it's not used these days.'

I look at the gate but it rings no bells. I'd love to be able to remember it, but the truth is I don't.

'The girls next door were called Caroline and Bryony. Caroline was older than us, but Bryony played here a lot, especially with my brother. Caroline was keen on domestic science. She went to the secondary school near mine, and sometimes I'd get a lift to school with her and her dad in his Volkswagen beetle.'

We unravel the mystery. Mrs Berrisford is the married name of Caroline. I find it surprising that she is still living round here, after all these years. It's something else I hadn't expected. We moved away. I thought everyone moved away.

I realise also that my confusion came from a generational shift that I had failed to catch up with. I was trying to relate Mrs Berrisford to Mr and Mrs Peel, on the assumption they were still in their middle age, as they were when I had last seen them. If they are still alive, I realise, they would be well into their eighties.

We continue our tour. We discuss the way in which the passage between the garage and the house was closed off. We go inside and discuss the solid fuel boiler that used to be in the corner of the kitchen. We discuss the other changes that have taken place: the kitchen and dining room are now one where they were two; there are stairs that never existed previously up to another floor that also did not exist; the sliding doors we had are of course gone, as is the raised bath so the hoist could get underneath; what was the bedroom where my dad's large hospital bed stood for those two years is now an extra living room; the entrance hall is enlarged. All is changed, all is unrecognisable from my past.

Or nearly all. There is one thing that I do perceive as remaining: in the room that used to be the bedroom I shared with my brother there is a strange combed pattern on the ceiling; this I remember vividly from the many hours I spent staring at it. The same pattern is also still in the living room.

As we return to the kitchen and I get ready to leave, I find myself telling my host more about the circumstances of my dad's accident. He listens well, and makes it possible. I try to express my thanks again.

'You know, I'm very grateful to have had the chance to look round. After my dad's accident, it was all such a difficult period in our family life. Coming to live here meant we could all be together again. It was very tough I think, while we were here, because of what had happened to my dad, but actually we also had some very happy times during those two years. I'm glad we had the chance to do that. It was just really, really hard when he died.'

I feel myself close to tears again. I don't really want to give way – in front of a relative stranger, however kind – so I struggle to keep myself on an even keel. I'm fairly good at it: been practicing for over forty years.

As we part he gives me directions to Caroline's house in case I want to call. I collect my bike, and set off, waving goodbye. I head down the hill to see the row of shops with the newsagents. I feel elated and excited. I have done what I had hoped to do. I have been back into the place of my dreams, and my nightmares, and I have survived.

I realise I never asked his name, or told him mine. I've been in a regressed state, which is not terribly surprising given the circumstances, and become more childlike. I'd forgotten what adults are supposed to do by way of introducing themselves. He hadn't seemed to mind. He had been a very accepting guide, and listener, and a feeling of gratitude, as well as elation, remains with me.

Past

At the bottom of the bank, where the row of shops should be, there are none. Instead a row of flats confronts me. The shops are gone, transformed into residences. I briefly try to imagine the development process that that would have entailed, and whether the shops went out of use through lack of business. Then I give up on that thought as an obsessional waste of time.

I find my way to where I think Caroline's house is. It's en route to where I'm going. But as I pause on the corner of her street, I realise I'm not inclined to call. I'm conscious of time now, and needing to push on if I am to fulfil my timetable for the day. And I'm still in the midst of the experience I've just had. I need to do justice to that, and savour it for a while. A little reluctantly, conscious also of the loss of what might have been, I move off.

Up the hill I used to walk to school along. Past the shop where we used to buy sweets like penny chews. An uncomfortable guilty feeling reminds me that we also indulged in shoplifting of a minor kind. I comfort myself by remembering that it was Charles, not me, who was the enthusiastic ringleader here - rather to my surprise at the time. Past the dentist's house, of horrid memory. Past the school playing field, where, at one time, groups of boys in my year got into the habit of chasing girls and pulling their knickers down. After a while they were all called in front of the headmistress, and told to desist. No guilt there, I wasn't part of that one.

The playing field is full of builders and machines. I ask a passing woman what's going on and she tells me they are building a replacement school. When it's finished, the old one will be demolished.

'But it only opened in 1960,' I say, amazed, as though it were yesterday, which is what it feels like. 'I went there when it first opened. What's wrong with it?'

'Well,' she says with a laugh. 'I guess they only built them with a limited lifespan. And now it's coming to an end.'

Past this school of so many memories – three years and two terms worth. Past the water tower, of dramatic appearance. Past the site of the old school annexe, where we spent most of our last year with Mr Still, and where Mrs Bray the headmistress came in briskly one day to read out the Eleven plus results. I got my passport to the grammar school, but then I expected to. So did some of my friends. Elizabeth Brown expected to, but she didn't, and she cried.

Past the fields where we used to play football at games time. I had football boots, with huge long laces that wrapped round and round. The games involved lots of boys all gathered round the ball trying to hack at it. It was more like a rugby ruck than football. If you did the correct thing and stayed out waiting for a pass, then your opportunities for contact with the ball itself approached zero.

Past Ireland Wood school which my brother and I went to for only three weeks, before our new one opened after Christmas. Michael Otley, a boy in the class with his own guitar, sang 'Living Doll.'

Past the bus stop where the boys from the secondary modern waiting for their bus to go home might attack me as I cycled past – I sometimes cycled to and from my grammar school in the warmer weather.

I take a left turn along a dual carriageway. I'm leaving the familiar realm of my childhood territory now, and the memories that go with it. Instead I'm in the realm of childhood Neverland. As a child, this is the road I never came along. These are the sights I never saw. This is the place I never came to. This, behind the iron gates, and the trees, and the big driveway, is the crematorium. This is where the funeral was. This is where his ashes are scattered.

Dinner date

There are mature trees, and plenty of them. They give the place a definite woodland feel, and I like that.

There is a large gothic-looking building, the crematorium itself. It seems to advertise an inflated sense of its own self-importance and I like that too.

There is a little building off to one side with books of remembrance, and toilets. I make use of one half of what's on offer, but not the other. A few cars and people are about, which suggests that a funeral is in progress, but if so it is a quiet one.

There is even a discreet, and rather ancient looking café. All is peaceful, which is, of course, how it should be.

I consult the little map in my notebook, and push my bike along the paths till I arrive at Upper Woodland Glade 1, Path 3.

I make myself at home on a rickety bench set back from the path. The bench is dedicated to two people called Poppy: Harold and Annie Poppy, from Filey, 'Reunited. February 1972.' The bench is overshadowed by a vigorous holly tree, which makes some of the bench a potentially prickly place to sit, but there is enough prickle-free room for me.

The sun is shining down through the leaves of the trees above me. Around me and stretching off into the distance in the Woodland Glade are flowers: some of them real, and some of them plastic. They sit in pots, and vases, and they lie on the ground, some still in their wrapping paper. They are mixed in with the autumn leaves, flashes of exotic brightness amongst the muted tones of decay.

I notice I am not feeling grief-struck, I am not feeling agitated, and neither am I feeling a great sense of peace. I am feeling, instead, rather cheerful; and also a little bit peckish.

I decide to have my dinner with my dad.

From my saddle bag I fetch my little repast, liberate it from the assorted plastic bags in which it is wrapped, and spread it out on the bench. Then, feeling peculiarly free to do what I choose, I wander off for a look round before I eat. Are there really ashes? Are there bits of bone visible?

There are mostly mementoes. Along the bevelled edges of the path, small metal plates are attached, hundreds of them, which record the people who once were, but are now no more. 'In memory of a loving wife and mother. Anne J Harker.' 'Happy memories of Harry Whiteside. Loved and missed by us all.' 'Forever loved.' 'A much loved father.'

And beyond the metal plates, and the path, there are, indeed, ashes. Patches of grey white material lie scattered amongst the grass, and leaves, and mementoes.

As I wander amongst the leaves, and the mementoes, and the ashes and the plastic tat, I realise I am feeling quite happy and relaxed. I have arrived. My dad's ashes are somewhere here. I have a right to be here, as much right as anyone, and more than most. Bereavement gives me a licence to roam – at least on Woodland Glade 1, Path 3.

As well as the flowers, people have left cards, and various plastic things, as offerings. In my present mood, I take it all in, and enjoy it all. People express their grief and love in their own way, and that is their right. Who am I to legislate on grief?

Some of the cards are written by people for whom writing by hand looks a bit of a struggle, their message all the more impressive for that: 'Thinking of you on father's day.' 'To Dad.' 'Dad, you are always in my heart.'

I like the two large words spelled out in green plastic material on frames propped up on the ground near each other: MAM and NAN. Traces of the original yellow flowers that they supported remain. A large patch of ashes is scattered nearby.

A large wicker basket sits near pots of flowers, plants trailing from it, and ribbons tied around it.

One memorial I particularly like features an arrangement of a small plastic gnome sitting on a toadstool, together with a stone model of a Miss Tiggy Winkle type hedgehog. There is also a small green and white spotted insect on a stick. These surround a card in blue. This is what I read on the card:

'Dad, I have so many great memories of good times we had when I was growing up, even though I'm grown and have a life of my own now. I still cherish the memories of those good times with you. So much of how I live my life and of who I am today is a result of your influence. You've always been one of the most important people in my life, and you still are. So even though we may not spend as much time together as we once did, I want you to know that you're always with me, right here in my heart, where you belong.'

I wander back to my bench and my lunch date with my dad. I munch contentedly on my food. I feel that I have permission to eat here in this place, that I am on safe ground. The permission comes from his death, which confers rights and privileges upon me as a member of his family. I can commune with my dad in whatever way is right for me, and no-one can gainsay me, let them try if they will. In this I have a sense of absolute authority.

It helps me realise how much, despite my efforts over the years to carve out my own sense of self, and my own scale of values, I am still in sway to the crowds around. Or perhaps more accurately, to my imagined version of their power and influence.

From there it is only a short step to realising that, as in grieving for my father, I have an authority to decide how I lead my life that is uniquely mine. I have a right to do in my life whatever is right for me. Death will come to me sooner or later. Better not wait too long for permission from someone else to get my life together. No special favours likely there.

Here, knowingly close to his mortal remains for the first time in my life, I do feel a sense of his presence, and it is helpful to me. He would have had my interests at heart, he would have supported me. He would have loved me if he had lived.

The wind is in the trees around me. There are mature oaks, and others I cannot recognise from my bench. The sky is clouding over, and it is getting chillier. I put my jumper on and also my overtrousers. I like it here. I'd like to stay a little more. I feel close to my dad, to his remains, and to his essence.

I start singing another of Leonard's songs: 'I'd like to say a little more... Oh, love went on and on; until it reached an open door, then love itself, oh love itself, was gone.'

Growing up without him, I missed his love. I also missed someone to joke with, someone to share a slightly private sense of humour with. We might have laughed together at the strange mixture of grief, sentiment, neglect and tat that fills this place. Not far from where I sit, someone has put into the ground a giant plastic yellow windmill in the shape of a buttercup. It's nothing to get worked up about, we might have said, and then chuckled together about it.

But strangely, at this moment missing him is not a big deal. I'm not cracked up about it. It's OK. It's how it is, it's how it was.

Dad, I say, I wonder what you would really have made of me, with my odd ideas, and not quite conventional life-style. Would you have been proud of me, and of what I've done in my life? Would you have liked me for my successes, and, perhaps more importantly, liked me when I failed?

I've missed out on those heavy-duty, important parts of the father-son thing: the heart-to-hearts, the advice, the confessions, the wisdom. But it's also the ordinary times I've missed. I would just have liked to talk to you about my day, and swap information, and compare notes. We could have watched TV together, or cooked food, or mended the shed roof. We could have argued over sport, or unsuitable girlfriends, or modern morals. I'm still just so sad that we never did all that.

But dad, we both know that's just how it was, and how it is, and always will be. Even so, right now I do feel a sense of your smiling presence. I'm grateful for that, and also for that time that we did have together: six years of your whole body and whole love, three years of your paralysed body and whole love. It's more than some get.

I'm getting a bit cold now. The sky is pretty grey, and I think it might rain soon. And I've got a good few miles to go before nightfall.

Well dad, I think it might be time for me to move on. Let's meet up again some time. I've really enjoyed my lunch with you today.

Solid rock

Back down the dual carriageway, singing 'Love went on and on' really loudly amongst the traffic, I hit childhood territories again. As I negotiate a huge, thoroughly dangerous roundabout, I know that on the other side of it is my old secondary school, also thoroughly dangerous. On trips through Leeds over the years I have passed it several times, and never without a shiver of anxiety and misery. I went there for only a year and a half before we moved away from the area, but that was a year and a half too long. An old-fashioned boys' grammar school, its rigid emphasis on uniform and uniformity, on deference and obedience, coupled with an ignored subculture of violence among the boys left its mark of fear and loathing upon me. I couldn't wait to get away at the end of each day, and I was delighted to leave it altogether. I was so happy, that when I told my friends the news, I forgot they might miss me, and I might miss them. To my surprise, Charles was upset, rather than happy, though he tried to hide it. Sorry Charles, there were times when I was not the best best-friend in the world.

As I cycle past, I look across the road towards the grim, Stalinist, thirties tenement-like block that I grew to hate. Instead I see light, modern, attractive buildings. The Stalinist block is no more. It has been knocked down. I am amazed and delighted, and give a cheer. I am sorry only to have missed the demolition, which I would have paid good gold to see. To think that all my childhood wishes for the place finally came true. Today is turning out well in all sorts of unexpected ways.

I am cycling the route that, as children, we used to take on the 33 bus from Cookridge to the centre of Leeds. En route I pass a place where we went to a barber who cut our hair, and, just round the corner, a cinema we went to that showed us films - like Swiss Family Robinson. I remember being excited at the time, going with Charles on his birthday as a treat, but I now know the film to be a terrible Disney distortion of a good story.

Getting closer to the city centre, I turn right off the main road, and enter a quiet tree-lined street. The somewhat dilapidated single-storey building set back a little from the road behind bushes and a gate is a children's nursery. I know it well. I spent 1983 coming here roughly one weekend every month to learn how to be a (post-) Reichian therapist. The opening circle of the first evening of the first weekend was also when I first saw Mary.

I take a picture of the place, in case Robbie or Rowan are interested in where their parents met. I'm not particularly convinced of the likelihood of this.

The person we were learning to be therapists from was William West, who became a good friend. He learned from someone called Peter Jones, who learned from Ola Raknes, in Norway, who learned from Reich himself. Reich learned from Freud. I always felt quite pleased with how short and direct the lineage was. Well, you Freudians in your book-lined studies amongst mature suburban streets, how short is your lineage?

Wilhelm Reich was one of Freud's favoured early protégées, who broke with him over issues like touch, and energy, and politics. In the eighties, those were the issues that particularly attracted us in our alternative cultural way, and we worked hard on touching people, and trying to release our blocked life energy, and developing radical politics. We didn't like Freud, well I didn't, because he was too wordy, and too straight, and too associated with mainstream, middle-class, money-making analysts. Actually, Reich was pretty wordy too, but as we didn't much believe in reading anything theoretical, that didn't matter a great deal. We preferred just to do it. We learned experientially.

And Reich was definitely not mainstream. Not with orgone accumulators, cloud busting, or aiming at orgastic potency. Or being thrown into prison in the States, and having your books burned on the orders of a federal agency, and then dying in gaol.

But for me, as for most of us, I think, the therapy thing was a deeply personal exploration, not a career move.

For example. I am in a large ramshackle loft area in an old warehouse in Sheffield as part of a therapy group. Scattered around the place are people in pairs or threes. We have been sent off for a period to do sessions with each other. I am lying on my back, feeling a bit lost, a bit stuck – the usual. Two women are helping me – to do what? Helping me breathe more, feel more, be more. Whatever comes up, they try to help it happen more so. At one point one of them tries a quick list of words on me to see what they trigger: 'love, mother, child, always, never...' It's 'never' that does it. I'm catapulted into grief and crying, and that impossible reality that 'never' attempts to describe, the reality which I know, but have covered over till now. Never see him again. Never hear him again. Never laugh with him again. Never. Never. Never. All so huge. Huge space where he has gone, and huge time that he has disappeared into. Not next year, not even in ten years' time, but never. It's all so huge, and I'm so small, and he's not here to help me deal with it, because I will never see him again.

It's horrible, and horribly scary and painful, and I am driven to go back into it. I want to know, I want to find out more, I want to understand, I want to know.

I'm willing to pay a big price in pain, because in the end, if I can get to it, the truth is a solid rock that I can stand on; whilst my held-down feelings, and my fear of them, is a morass into which I sink anew each day.

Just badness

Back into the traffic stream, which in this case is stationary, dammed up by traffic lights way down the road. The afternoon is now quite warm, and a young man sits in his car, the window open and loud music playing. I cycle past him, and my inner music machine loudly churns out some more Leonard Cohen. I am confident that mine, though less technically proficient, is the healthier, more life-affirming version. Reich would have approved. Feeling suitably self-satisfied, I move steadily forward with the increased pleasure of the peculiarly acute kind that overtaking a long line of stationary traffic brings to any cyclist.

At the traffic lights I recognise the way to an old church hall nearby where I also did several weekends with William. I realise I did a lot of therapy back then. I liked it, I liked the people, I liked the group dynamics, even when they scared me.

In that hall we did a series of three linked weekends. Towards the end of one of the early ones, I announced that I was sorry, but that I was going to have to leave early, and I hoped that was OK with everyone. We were sitting in a circle. One of the women, sitting across from me, quickly responded.

'No it's not OK,' she said, 'Not with me.'

Slightly shocked, and confused, I made my excuses and left. I struggled with it all week. Why had she said that? What did she not like about me? How had I offended her? My younger, more polite, and more naive self devoted a large chunk of my weekly therapy session to the incident.

At the next weekend, summoning up my courage, I faced her across the circle, reminded her of the incident, and asked what it was about.

Oh that,' she said in an off-hand way, 'Oh that was just badness.'

I'm now moving past Woodhouse Moor, where funfairs were held when I was a child, and possibly still are. This gives way to the university. Now just over there, behind those buildings, is another place where I went on a weekend. This time it was years later, a final therapy hurrah, when Mary and I left the children with my mother for two days, and went together.

Past the university and I enter on to a series of roads, leading right into the city, where cycle lanes and signed cycle routes and certain privileged junction crossings provide me with an exhilarating but safe-ish dash into the centre. Here I manage to lose the cycle lanes, the protected status, and the way back to the canal. After a confusing trek through pedestrianised shopping streets, along a revamped river walkway, along dual carriageways, and through a giant weapons museum grounds, I hit a recognisable canal towpath, and breathe a trifle easier.

Green stuff is growing on the banks and verges: grass and bushes and trees, setting off the brick red of the old Leeds warehouses lined up on the other bank, and the red brick of the new waterside apartment blocks that are replacing them. The canal here is wide, and my study of the map suggests that what I am alongside is actually the river, which has here joined forces with the canal, though they separate again further downstream. In pursuit of the bifurcation, I set off eastwards.

Only a short distance along, after passing underneath a flyover for a giant roadway, a compulsory diversion away from the river-canal takes me through a decayed industrial area of boarded up factories and empty building plots. Feeling rather put out by this, I am reassured when I am signposted back to the canal-river via a special wooden trackway built to carry bikes right up against the boundary fence of a giant works. This turns out to be a Trade Team Excel Depot, with many of their excelling wagons parked up neatly round the back.

I find that the bifurcation point is about where I am, and I am presented once more with a canal and a river. The tow path lies on the other side of the canal, across the locks that provide entry from the river into the canal. We lucky cyclists have been provided with a specially constructed bike bridge to get to the other side.

In order to enable bikes to ascend to the relevant height to cross the canal, ramps rather than steps have been provided, and in order that these may be of a rideable gradient, yet squeezed into a reasonable space, they have been built as a zigzag, with three doglegs and two tight 180 degree turns. I make it to the top without stopping, or putting my feet down, or holding on to the sides, and feel suitably impressed with myself for doing so.

Moving on, I am travelling again, as I did this morning, between the canal on my right, and the river on my left. The breeze is again from behind me, and, the lunchtime rain threat having quietly disappeared, the autumn sun is shining, and a few high white clouds checker the blue sky. The canal now, however, is a significant waterway, designed, I imagine, to carry significant traffic from the sea to the heart of the industrial areas of Leeds.

I am content to pedal along the towpath, as the industrial heritage drops away, and scrub trees and bushes spread out from the river-canal basin, providing a sheltering belt of near-wilderness close to the middle of a big industrial city. I see only a handful of people.

The cycle way diverts me from one bank of the canal to the other via a minor road bridge, then back to the other side via another bridge. Here an unexpected challenge is provided by a steep flight of steps from the road down to the towpath. I cannot believe that this is the cycleway and cast about for the proper way down. But there is no other, easier, route further on. This is the one. Managing this with a fully-laden bike proves very difficult. It's hard to use the brakes to hold it back as I might on a road. The bike threatens to run away with me, and leave us both in a crumpled heap at the bottom. I end up half carrying the thing down, which leaves my shoulder sore. Where are the clever ramp systems when you really need them?

My daddy

Discovering therapy was like discovering a new world full of clever ramp systems. They could get me out of my stuck place on to a new level of reality where I could make progress. Systems, tools, approaches, and methods were available to be learned, read about, invented, and tried out. Some worked for me, some didn't. Some worked at one time and not at another. Some needed other people, some I could do on my own.

It probably starts with Roger, a friend when I was in my mid-twenties, who's read a book on self-hypnosis, and asks if I want to try it out. I lie on the bed in my attic bedroom in Birmingham, and he takes me through a process of relaxation of my body, and deepening of my breathing. It's essentially what I would now call a guided visualisation or meditation. He invites me to go back in my memory to earlier and earlier times. I'm fascinated by the process, and by the vivid scenes that come back.

I recall, for example, that when I was about five, my mother suggested one morning that I might like breakfast outside in the sunshine. I recall my surprise and excitement at this novel proposal, and wanting to do it. My mother put out a little stool for me to use as a table, and I sat outside in the warm early morning summer sunshine, and ate my breakfast from it. The stool was a box with a top that came off in which we kept shoe cleaning stuff. I had forgotten all about it, but Roger's process enables me to bring it back. I'm amazed. How can something get buried and 'forgotten', and then re-emerge with such clarity? I recall the top of the box, covered with a dark brown leather-like material to make a soft seat cover. I can feel the warmth of the sunshine on my skin, the brightness of the light, and the sense of peace and safety.

And I'm fascinated also by what doesn't come back. I realise for the first time how few memories I have of my father before his accident. This is an important realisation because I have a strong feeling alongside this that there is something wrong with this. This is not what I would have expected. I had assumed that my memory banks would be as chock full of father memories as they are of other memories. They don't seem to be.

Where do I go next with this? How do I find out more about my own history, about my own self?

I realised I didn't know who I was or where I was, so I cast about for clues, and a year or so later find myself in a room in a semi-derelict terrace high on the moors in the Pennines. Sitting on the floor facing me close by is Mike, his soft brown eyes registering concern and quiet confidence. He's done this before and I trust him.

He's there to support me, and he is supporting me: I feel it. Later on it will be my turn to support him, but right now we are concentrating on me. I can vaguely hear the voices of other pairs of men in other rooms doing the same thing. I am talking about my dad, and how I felt when he died. I am remembering my bedroom as a child, and my mum coming in. Mike is listening carefully and sympathetically. He gets me to repeat certain phrases. He encourages me to say them louder.

'It was just so horrible. I feel so bad. I miss him.'

'Try saying that again, tell me again.'

'It was just so horrible. I just really, really, miss him.'

I can feel it all start to build in me. I've never talked to anyone about it before who wants to know more, who wants me to go deeper, and who isn't afraid of my grief. Mike is still concerned, but he is not afraid, or embarrassed, and I can feel that. I can really feel that. I am very sensitive to it. He is creating with me a space in which I feel emotionally safe, and he is helping me allow the force of my emotions so that they can emerge, and enter that space.

I start to sniffle, and my eyes burn, and tears start to come.

Mike is not only unphased by this, he encourages me.

'Let them come. Let the tears come. Let the sounds come. It's OK to do that.'

I start to cry seriously. My eyes screw up, and I hear myself sobbing, and I feel my nose running furiously. Mike is pushing paper hankies in my hand. But he is still being encouraging, and his confident presence is like magic.

'It's OK to cry. Just let it happen. Let the sounds come.'

I do let the sounds come. It hurts physically. My chest hurts, my throat is tight and raw, my nose hurts, my screwed up eyes hurt. I hear wailing sounds, and the rawness of the grief emerging from me is shocking, but the sounds tell me that there is a hurt person making them, and that the grief of this person is real. This brings a renewed rush of energy and tears and sounds. Grievous energy comes up from the depths of me, and bursts out of all the exits it can find: salt tears from my eyes, snot from my nose, sobs from my lungs, and sounds from my mouth.

'Just let it happen. Keep breathing.' I hear Mike, his voice now a little shaky, but still determinedly encouraging me, and I feel him too, bending over my kneeling body, and holding me lightly. I have permission. I have permission. I have support. 'Try telling him direct,' he says, 'try speaking to him.'

'Daddy, Oh daddy. Don't leave me, don't leave me. Please come back, please.'

I hear the words I have never heard before, because I have never said them out loud before. I hear the desperation and misery in them. I hurt, I hurt all over, and I hurt all inside. The words, the despair, the misery, it all keeps coming up, and out.

'My daddy, my daddy, my daddy... he's gone, he's gone... come back, please come back... don't leave me here without you... I want you so much.'

My crying hits a crescendo; I am not in control and I am scared, but Mike is there, and that makes it just bearable.

And then it starts to fade, and die away, and gradually, gradually I come back to the room and myself. My sobs quieten down. My throat is raw, and my eyes are sore from the crying. I lie quietly while Mike covers me with a blanket, and holds my hand, and I blow my nose.

And after a while something else strange and unexpected happens. I realise I'm no longer feeling sore and in pain. Instead I feel deeply OK. I seem to breathe easier than I've ever breathed before. Mike looks wonderful, and I feel relaxed enough to smile and laugh with him. He brings me a cup of tea, and we hang out together for a while, talking it over.

Later, when we all go outside, my eyes are still puffy and sore, but the world is sparkling, and bright. I see detail that my short-sightedness normally hides from me. I pick out the individual bricks on the walls of the bottom terrace fifty yards away.

The others look at me, and smile, and then look in my eye and tell me I have burst a little blood vessel so that red blood has spread over part of one of my eyeballs.

For the next few days, until it gradually fades away, Donovan, a sweet little Dutch-Australian boy who is living with us in this place, is fascinated by my appearance, and constantly asking me to bend down so he can have another look at my marked eye. I always agree, and smile into his beautiful eyes a few inches away from mine, while, slightly anxiously, he glances from one of my eyes to the other and tries to comprehend the strangeness of the sight before him.

Sean

I am cycling in a wide shallow valley. The canal, broad and wind-ruffled, is on my right. Further away to my left is the river. Low scrubby trees fill most of the visible space. Above me, a high, wide, blue sky with a few scurrying white clouds signifies endless space and time. No other person is in evidence.

I took my therapy seriously. Every week I went along to a run-down terraced house in Sheffield, locked my bike up in the backyard, and waited in the downstairs room till whoever was before me upstairs was finished. Sometimes it was the lady who stood silently for a few seconds, holding her cash and blessing it before handing it over to Sean.

Sean was our therapist. He'd done the training before me, and had been working for a while. Sean worked near where I lived: he was available. I started on the journey with him.

I'd go upstairs to the attic room and lie down. Sean would sit nearby, and I would breathe. Sometimes he would press on my chest to amplify my breathing, or press on my jaw muscles or other tight spots on my body. Sometimes he would give me instructions to look at him, or follow his moving finger with my eyes. Sometimes we would talk.

Sometimes it was all low key and sensible. Sometimes it was a wild emotional rollercoaster of a ride through grief and anger, and joy and fury. Sometimes insight and understanding would flow and all would make sense; and sometimes it was more of a mess at the end than it had been at the beginning.

Afterwards, I would pay him my money, cycle home, and write up my notes about the session. I was serious about my therapy. I studied myself, and studied the therapy journey, as I've always studied anything I find new and fascinating.

We explored relationships, and sex and love, and friendships. We explored my physical health and the workings of my body. We explored my attitudes and my values, and the ways in which I understood the workings of the world: some of them hidden from me, some of them strange, some of them strange and hidden. We looked at my children and the ways I related to them. We covered the full gamut of my emotional life: what I came to see as the four main ingredients of sadness and fear and anger and joy. And all the subdivisions and curious mixtures: jealousy and envy; shame and remorse and guilt; longing and desire; sneering contempt and punishing coldness; worry and anxiety and a deep sense of unease; hope, all kinds of hope: optimistic hope, naïve hope, hopeless hope.

We covered and uncovered childhood experiences. And we kept coming back to my dad. No matter how much I cried, no matter how scary it was, no matter how much I tried to avoid it – we kept coming back to my dad.

And some of it was totally unexpected. I had expected the grief, the pain of loss, and the pain of missing him. Something different happened one time as I lay on Sean's mattress, in Sean's attic, with a grey winter afternoon sky dimly visible through the skylight. Sean had been poking and prodding me as was his wont. He had been making me breathe more deeply. The theory was that breathing more deeply raised your energy levels. Your raised energy then tried to flow more strongly and came up against your blockages, your resistances. The therapist's job was then to work with those resistances until they dissolved, or until the energy blasted them away.

Sean is making me talk to my dad directly, as though he is there. It starts off, as these things usually do, on familiar territory. 'Well, dad, I miss you, you know. You're not here anymore, and well, it's not the same without you. That accident did for you, and it did for us too, it did for me. Why did it happen?'

Sean encourages me to keep talking to my dad, to keep breathing.

'What were you doing having an accident?' I hear myself start to complain. 'You were supposed to be an expert, a top PT instructor. What were you doing diving into a swimming pool and hitting your head on the bottom. That's not very clever, is it? What was going on? What did you think you were doing?'

I hear to my surprise a rising crescendo of anger in my voice. Sean is encouraging me to let it out, and poking me in painful places. I'm not expecting to be angry with my dad, but I am. I'm not supposed to be angry with him, but I am. He needs my love and sympathy, not my anger. I've never heard anyone ever get angry with him - he was paralysed for God's sake. He was a victim. He was vulnerable. People looked after him. I looked after him.

I try and hold my anger back, but it's too late, for Sean and I have created the open space, and Sean is still encouraging me to let it out, not hold it back, and then there's no more control as a torrent of fury and anger spews out of me. 'You stupid man, you fucking careless bastard, hitting your fucking head on the bottom, what sort of stupid fucking stupid thing is that, look what you did.' And I'm rolling around on the mattress in a fury, hitting out at the cushions and the mattress with my fists, and screaming and shouting. 'Left us here, because you weren't looking what you were doing. You had no fucking right to do it. You should have looked, you should have looked, you should have looked. You left us here, you left us behind. Don't do it. For Christ's sake look what you're doing...don't go, don't go, don't go.'

And then I'm crying again, because it always seems to end in tears, and I'm lying on my front on this mattress in this strange room, with my eyes screwed shut, sobbing quietly, and my dad is dead, and has been for such a long time, and I haven't seen him or felt him for so long. I feel my body shake rhythmically with my sobs, and I feel Sean's hand gently touching me on my back.

Herod's Army

Just before I leave the canal, which at this point is very wide, I pause at a bench. I've enjoyed these last few miles through industrial wasteland-cum-wilderness. There has been a wide sky, a fresh breeze to blow the clouds along, and an absence of people – three bonuses to be grateful for. I recall with gratitude also, the help I received in my therapy journey from friends along the way. In this respect, and at this moment, William feels the key figure: his caring, his calmness, his confidence that matters could be resolved and healed; plus his sense of humour, his sense of fun and his terrible jokes. 'Well done, William', I think, 'thanks for it all.'

Those workshops in strange church halls and children's nurseries, the techniques he brought, and the humanity, those were some of the keys to unlocking the grief and sadness dammed up in my being. Energy, like water, and grief, (and God) moves in mysterious ways, and when it moves it can be simply beautiful. At this moment, I know it is all energy, it's all energy in the end, and it's all beautiful.

I check my watch, and see I have about three hours till dark, and about twenty miles to go to make Selby, my intended resting place. I haven't booked anywhere to stay, convinced that at this time of year there will be no-one staying anywhere. In my current mood, I'm confident of finding somewhere, and of making it before dark. Panic and anxiety are well under control, (where will I stay tonight, what if there's no room, what if I have to sleep in a gutter, in the cold and dark?) and its going to be rainbows, rainbows all the way.

I leave the safety of the canal, and brave the dangers of the road once more. It is not only me who finds the dangers apparent. In the next village, a little settlement called Swillington, the village fathers (or maybe mothers) have not been content to erect a conventional sign entreating drivers to 'please drive carefully'. No, their sign goes a step further: 'Spare our children', it says, then adds 'please drive carefully', and finally, 'Thank you'. I chuckle morbidly at the thought that the local parish council has recognised the true purpose of our modern transportation system: to mow down all the innocents, like some latter day Herod's army. Will their plea make a difference? I hope so, but have my doubts.

At the far end of the village I can get off the main road, which is very busy, and noisy and stinking, and which I hate. The relief at being in a sane environment is immense. The minor road I am now on is surrounded by ploughed fields, and I can smell the soil. I move on cartographically too – on to a different map. I check back: I've been following this map since this time yesterday. And I'll follow the new one till sometime tomorrow. A map a day helps you cycle, rest, and pray.

On this new map I have marked nearby the course of an off-road cycle route, and I work my way towards it. I find it in the bottom of a cutting crossing the road I'm on, and I detour into the depths to find the level route of an old railway line. My stately progress takes me eventually past fields and housing estates, where groups of children, recently released, make their way home from school, and seem reasonably good tempered about it. One of the fields has a mysterious small fire lit in the middle of it, and some of the children, not unnaturally, take more than a passing interest.

At one stage, I am about to overtake a young man walking with his head down. Not wanting him to be shocked I warn him of my presence, as kindly as I can. He looks up at me as I pass, and his face seems to me to convey such misery that I am deeply affected. I want to do something, but I do not stop, for fantasy is one thing, and my capacity to act with authenticity in the world is another. But this is the fantasy that I immediately have: I stop him and tell him, 'You are sad. You are not being loved properly. Look me in the eyes. You are loveable. Not being loved properly does not make you bad.' That does not feel a difficult thing to do, but it does feel an impossible thing to do. Surely, if we had the will, we could all of us do that for someone?

An example of someone telling me a truth that was helpful to me: I used to have supervision sessions on my work as a therapist. The supervisor was an older woman who was a counsellor. She very gamely tried to make sense of some of the more outré theoretical and practical aspects of the Reichian-type therapy I was doing at the time, and the knots I was tying myself in. We had been discussing my father's accident, and the wrestling bouts I was having with myself trying to make it have a meaning, looking for a cause, looking for antecedents, or contributory factors in my behaviour as a child, or in my parents' relationship, or in the zeitgeist of the times. After a while she looked at me very directly and paused, and then said, very slowly and distinctly, 'You know, sometimes an accident is just an accident.'

Sailing

I come down off my now elevated old railway line on to a road again. In order to access the road I have to manoeuvre my bike through another clever metal stile arrangement designed to let me through but prevent the passage of my motorised bicycle acquaintances. Ah, the glorious feeling of privilege. Above me, an endearing metal sculpture of a steam train in silhouette complete with steam and signal announces that the path I have just traversed is called 'The Lines'.

Blown along again by the wind, I pass a nature reserve situated around an area of open water. My own nature is in ascendant mood as I experience a wonderful ride, with cut fields on each side, and a rainbow in front of me. The rainbow is the latest, and the best, in a long series today. This one does not fade away, but stays, and stays, a lovely low half circle in the sky before me. It is not fixed in its appearance, but melts and melds with the sky and air and colours around, now fading a little, now getting brighter. Keeping me company on my journey, I cannot help but keep it in my sight for an extended period, longer than I've ever observed one before. I know it is, traditionally, a symbol of harmony, and I feel it affecting me. I am struck by its ethereality. It cannot be grasped; it is not matter, but only energy, translated into, and visible as, colour.

And under the spell of this wonderful fresh phenomenon, that cannot be grasped, or owned, or privileged to a few, an insight emerges for me: I have as much right to be in the world as anyone else – no more, no less; I have as much right to life as anyone else – no more, no less.

It is a peculiarly satisfying thought. I feel safer, and stronger, now that it has appeared. As I examine it, I start to feel it embed itself within me. I recognise also that it can only have the power that it does because I did not previously recognise those rights. However, as with many experiences of insight, I had not previously been aware that anything was missing. I connect the lack with growing up without a father, feeling that something was wrong with me, that I was handicapped, that I did not have the same rights as others to be in the world: those other boys, with their confidence, and their big boots, and their live fathers to back them up. Now the experience in the crematorium, the sense of authority that death has given back to me, has wrought a change within. The rainbow has exerted a pull on the new harmony within and brought out of me the promise of a better balance with the world. I cannot grasp the rainbow, but it is not too late to grasp my rightful place in the scheme of things; no more, or less, than anyone else.

I thankfully get myself over the maelstrom that is the dual-carriagewayed A1(T) by means of a pedestrian bridge. On the other side, peace returns along unfenced roads running between cut fields under late afternoon autumn sunshine. I cross a bridge and look down on an elongated construction site. A great swathe of churned-up country stretching into the distance is the subject of attention by various men in hard hats and their various machines. One side of the cutting is clothed in a glorious flat length of unused tarmac at least three lanes wide that disappears unto the horizon. Guys, I say, it's really great of you to make such a beautiful cycleway, but really, six inches is all we cyclists need. Get things in perspective, think of the earth's resources.

The sun is warm on my back, on this Indian summer evening, and the wind is strong at my back as my progress continues towards the east. A long, flat road, stretching ahead between cut fields of grain, with occasional distant trees and copses, is my prospect. The horizon is distant, and the sky feels huge. The powerful wind makes progress almost effortless. I quickly reach a certain speed and I stop pedalling. I stand up on the pedals like a mast, and hold out one side of my coat to catch the wind like a sail, and I am blown on, and on, and on, only slowly slowing down to the point where I start the process again.

An enormous and convenient village green provides a resting space, and I hear the wind thrashing in the branches of a tall Lombardy poplar above me as I sit and admire the old brick-built, pantile-roofed farmhouses around me. Money, and the moneyed classes that go with it, has moved into the area, and created its usual rash of facsimiled cottages, paved parking areas, conservatories and suburban gardens.

The next half-mile provides an illuminating new angle on the power of the wind. The road heads north-west before turning east again, and even though I am not heading directly into the wind, its force makes progress a complete struggle. I remain in a low gear, and am fighting hard. The ploughed and harrowed field on my right has a mist at ground level, where the fine particles of soil are being picked up, blown along, and deposited somewhere else. I realise that my journey is only possible because I am headed east. The reverse direction could only be achieved at the cost of an enormous ongoing battle with the wind. It would be a battle in which I would suffer rapid defeat.

Trial

Approaching Selby, I have the task of finding somewhere to stay for the night. In my pannier, I have a list of the names and addresses and phone numbers of several guest houses, gleaned from the internet before I left. Preferring not to hamstring myself, I have not booked in advance. I am going to 'confidently feel my way into something that will be right for me': cue hollow laughter from my internal sceptic.

I locate the banks of the Selby canal, and for the last mile or so approach the town centre via the towpath. Amongst the canal boats moored on the far bank is one named 'Therapy'. Surely a good omen. Selby announces itself with a magnificent abbey in its centre, all gothic towers of yellow stone glowing in the early evening light. I like it so much that my immediate thought is that I must stay somewhere close by. I look out for suitable accommodation. There is a hotel within spitting distance, of the old fashioned posting house variety, but I decide it is beyond my budget for the trip. I wander the streets nearby, but find nothing. I cycle the streets and roads a little further away, and find nothing. The traffic noise and bustle is getting me down. It is getting late. The cold gutter prospect is looming large in my consciousness, along with a sense of failure – a failure that would not be countenanced by proper men from, for example, the navy. I try even further off, but find nothing. I am getting cold. I find a bed and breakfast place, but don't like the look of it, so go off and search a bit more. I don't find anything. I don't ask anyone for help, because I'm not that kind of guy: I'm a regular guy, who doesn't need help. I'm not panicking. I am not panicking. I go back to the place I didn't like the look of, and ring the bell. 'Sorry,' says the young woman who answers, 'I let my last room five minutes ago. If only you'd come a bit earlier.' I finally ring some of my numbers. They are full, or don't answer, or don't do accommodation any more. I go back into the town centre, and notice the original hotel again. I notice it is right by the abbey that I like so much. I re-examine my budget, and decide, in a flash of inspiration and confidence, that the budget can be stretched. I chain my bike to a drainpipe and go in. I enquire at the reception desk, and they have room. I do not collapse in relief on the floor, or attempt to embrace the receptionists, but pretend that this is the most normal occurrence in the world. I enquire about accommodation for my bike, and this also can be arranged. I accept the offer of a newspaper in the morning with my breakfast. They ask what I would like for breakfast, and I confess that I do not eat meat or dairy or eggs. The two women there look at each other and exclaim that they have 'never heard of that one before', but at this juncture I would forgive them anything.

Later, my bike safely stashed away in an outhouse, I relax in my perfectly nondescript room, and allow the panic (which I did not have) to drain away from my body. I make myself some tea. I draw the net curtains so that the wonderful view of the upper parts of the abbey about fifty yards away, which dominates the window, can be more clearly enjoyed, and I do enjoy it. I have achieved my wish, and I have felt my way into something right, but it has been by a very torturous, anxious, and non-confident route. This is my old and familiar style: to get round things as best I can, on the fringes, making do. If my insight on having an equal right to be in the world had been fully functioning within me, then I would have immediately recognised the hotel as the perfect solution to my dilemma, and saved myself the slough of despond in between. So still some work to do there then. Bloody hell, dad, where were your wise words when I needed them? I retire to soak in the bath and lick the wounds of my skirmish with Selby, my trial by accommodation.

Selbyville

Breakfast, at a very early hour, and in a seemingly windowless and dark back dining room, is an exclusively male affair. Half a dozen of us sit at our little tables alone, while four of us double up. We read our papers. Mine, perused over a plate of fried mushrooms and tomatoes on toast (solved 'that one' quite easily) tells me, for example, that today's children are missing out on free-range play areas compared to my own childhood. "A typical eight-year-old's 'home habitat' – the area that children are allowed to travel around on their own – has shrunk by 90% over the last thirty years, according to Tim Gill, the director of the Children's Play Council. An average eight-year-old is now allowed to stray only within a hundred yard circumference of the front door, the council's research showed... Mr Gill warned that a combination of 'stranger-danger' fears, public intolerance of youngsters playing outside, and the lack of official spaces was leading to the extinction of the 'outside child.'"

While I digest this relevant little snippet and sip some fruit juice, I contemplate my activities of the previous evening. After due consideration, I have to acknowledge that my accommodation skirmish with Selby was not the end of my errors of judgement. Once recovered from my bath I had gone out in search of sustenance. I could have bought some tempting and healthy morsels from the local supermarket and taken them back to my room to eat in comfort and privacy. But no, I did the normal thing and went in search of a hostelry where I might be looked after and find convivial company (more hollow laughter and 'I told you that would never work' from my internal sceptic, who has grown bolder since being proved right over the accommodation debacle). Given my awkward diet, I was fortunate, in Selby, on a weekday autumn evening, to find anything at all. The establishment favoured with my custom was an Indian restaurant. It was a large establishment. There were five of us in there. The clientele here was also an exclusively male affair. Three young men were trying to celebrate the birthday of one of them. Their method of choice for celebrating was, without much grace or humour, to take the piss out of each other, especially out of the birthday boy. The other lone man, and myself, at our widely separated tables, appeared not to be celebrating anything. An exercise in conviviality it was not. It could instead be accurately described as an excellent example of how to feel really lonely without in any way trying.

The light was too dim to read by, and so I was forced to take notice of my surroundings.

Neither did the food redeem the occasion. The pakoras were tasteless, the dahl was watery and flavoured exclusively with garlic. I did not complain: I'm a regular guy and we don't do that. We've been well trained by generations of school dinner ladies to eat what's put in front of us and be grateful for it. Faced with the increasing external pressures of rubbish food demanding to be eaten, and the increasing internal pressures of indigestion and a rising sense of impotence and humiliation, I reverted to type and old habits: I panicked. Realising I could escape if I acted quickly, I paid the bill and ran. In my haste I was also overcharged, but at the time it seemed a small price to pay for a quick exit.

I walked back through the dark and empty streets of Selby. I was now referring to it in my own mind as Selbyville, in a joshing kind of reference to the Simpson's neighbouring town of Shelbyville. Shelbyville was founded so that the original settlers could marry their cousins - though I'm sure the upright citizens of Selbyville would want to do no such thing. I wondered what my next error might be, and how come I still hadn't learned to run all my life on a sensible basis.

In my room, I turned on the telly to channel flick for a few minutes, and got hooked by a programme explaining how all the Abba songs came to be written. It was not a terrible programme, there are just better things you can spend doing on an evening already half-ruined. The songs are so catchy I just had to see how the next one came into being, and they wrote such a lot of them…

As I finish my breakfast, I wonder if I will ever really transform my obsessive impotent inner behaviour patterns, or whether it's always going to be a question of damage control. I am recognising more than ever this feeling that I have to apologise for my existence, to cower in corners, that I have no right to take part in what other people take for granted, that there is some deep sense of shame intrinsically bound up in being alive. I link this in large part to my father's death, but I do not really know how large a part his death may have played, or how large a part may be due to other family or childhood influences. It may even be that what I feel in these circumstances is 'normal', but if that is the case then everyone else is keeping pretty quiet about it. At least recognising it is a step along the road to dealing with it.

I recall, how, after he died, everything was grey, lifeless and empty. I had a powerful yearning to join him again, but I knew that could only happen when I myself was dead. I had somehow to get through the rest of my life without him, and my lifetime, for a young boy, seemed an impossibly infinite time: a life sentence.

Later still, as an adult, in one of those simple but inspired therapeutic moments, somebody, in the right way, and with the right timing, and the right sensitivity, did me the favour of asking me what my dad would have wanted for me. By now a father myself, I knew the answer immediately: he would have wanted me to get on and live my life as fully and joyfully as possible, and would be in pain if he thought my grieving over him was casting such a shadow over my life. So simple! It was a revelatory moment, and like all revelatory moments it seemed so obvious afterwards.

Now all can be solved, all can be harmony... If only insight were enough! But insight on its own is not sufficient to bring change, though it is a part of change. There's more work to do in terms of catching the old habits at their jobs, and persuading them to go into retirement, or take on a different responsibility. It's a long process, with much possibility of backsliding, because the habits go back a long way: they are deep rooted.

My highlight yesterday had been, I feel, the visit to the crematorium, and the lunch date with my dad. I had broken through old habits of taboo, and started to create new, more life-affirming ones. I don't have to be cut off so completely from my dad any more. Conversations with my dad are not any more forbidden or impossible – I can consider him available to me. We can be quite casual together: 'Hi dad' said in the same mock whiney American accent with which my daughter sometimes opens her conversations with me.

One of the practices that Thich Nhat Hanh recommends is, as you are meditating, to embrace, take in, and love, all those parts of yourself that you notice arising in your awareness. This is particularly important for those parts of yourself that you don't like, that you have learned to push away and ostracise. How can you be happy, or effective in the world, if you are spending your energy on keeping parts of yourself at bay, treating them like enemies? So now, when I notice my sense of humiliation, or shame, or feeling of inadequacy or panicky anxiety, I try to welcome and embrace them with compassion as old friends, as part of me. This is both very simple, and profoundly difficult, because it is dealing differently with deeply rooted habit energy. But if I succeed, then something magical starts to happen: the panic, or the shame, or whatever, dissolves or transforms, and, for a period, I have a sense of liberation of well-being and of peace.

I collect my bike and pack away my belongings. Outside I pass an old man pushing his bike along the street. Tied to his cross bar with string is his walking stick. I wonder how, if he needs a stick to walk with, he's going to manage riding his bike. We are headed in different directions, however, and so this remains an unsolved mystery.

I take myself into the grounds of the abbey nearby, and examine some of the graves. In the seventeenth and eighteenth centuries they had a different style in their expressions of loss. Here's the gravestone tribute to Ann Savage, who died in 1790, aged sixty-three:

Under this stone doth lie bereaved of life
An attendant mother and tender wife
A kind relation and enduring friend

Beloved in life, lamented at her end.

Navy

I leave Selbyville by following the course of a levee high above the river Ouse on my right, and also high above a terrace of houses on my left. They must have a great view of a large bank of earth towering above them. I wonder how often they go out to check river levels in times of flood, and then perhaps go back inside to check their house insurance premium levels.

After a couple of miles which provide increasing opportunities to admire the classic clean construction lines and effortlessly subtle siting of the Drax power station, my route leaves the levee and dawdles inland via an old driveway tunnelling its way through overhanging trees. Thoughtful planners have provided a genuine cycleway to help deal with the potential traumas of approaching a main road, and I note with approval the special signs with pictures of bikes on. The cycleway is a dual carriageway type: half for us cyclists, and half for pedestrians, our uneasy allies in the traffic wars. Width of carriageway is quite generous – a couple of feet rather than the six inches we can actually manage with. Fortunately, I meet no pedestrian en route, and, after a short while, I head off through a small village, with its typical small village church, and re-join the river.

Here, my route stays on the landward side of the levee so that I have no view of the river, unless I climb to the top. This I do at one point, curious about shouting men's voices that I can hear. Drax looms a mile or so away, but on the opposite river bank, some kind of large landing stage, all girders and bricks and brightly shining arc lights, is the subject of some unspecified attention for a group of workmen, bellowing and laughing at each other.

Passing on, I start to wonder about my dad and the navy. I know he joined up in 1937, when he was sixteen. Why did he join? I've always assumed it was to do with Hull being near the sea, and his father having been in the services, and job opportunities being restricted at the tail end of the thirties depression. But I realise I don't actually know. His older brother, Robbie, was also in the navy, and presumably joined first - perhaps that was an incentive. And what was it like leaving home at sixteen to join perhaps hundreds of other young lads at the navy's training establishment? Was it a harsh regime, or did they have a lot of fun? I have an impression that the navy is less punitive and bullying in its training methods than the army, but I don't know, and can no longer ask. I have one photo of a group of lads in shorts and singlets, on their knees scrubbing the floor in a building. Some look curiously at the camera. They seem neither cowed nor excited.

My dad loved sports of all kinds, and the navy would have provided opportunities to keep playing. I have photos of him, later on in his navy career, in football, rugby, cricket and hockey teams. He was also successful in diving competitions, as well as doing swimming, and of course gymnastics. He took part in several royal tournaments, doing complicated synchronised gymnastic displays in a window framework sixty feet above the ground, or training the group of men to do spectacular vaults, or handstands on dining chairs balanced on their two back legs.

And my mum, how did she come to be in Hull so that she could meet my dad, so that they could get married, and have me and my brother? These are my origins, and it all feels important, and a little unlikely.

Her family originally came from Brampton, near Carlisle, where they had lived, as far as I can trace back, for generations. She, the eighth of nine children, was born in northern France on Boxing Day in 1919, because her father, a quartermaster in the army (he'd joined up for wartime service), was still employed there sorting out surplus material after the war. He had brought over his wife and some of the younger children to be with him.

When my mother was three, and back in Brampton, her own mother died in childbirth, bleeding to death, with the new-born child dying with her. My grandfather was now, aged thirty-nine, left a widower with nine children. The younger children were farmed out to various relatives. My mother went to live her mother's brother Ned, and his wife Sally, an older couple who were themselves childless.

Life with her Aunt Sally was where my mother's earliest memories start. It seems, from her reports and stories, to have been on the whole a fair upbringing, but rather strict. As a child I was taken on several occasions to Brampton to visit Sally, and her eccentric sister Elizabeth, two old ladies whose house always smelled strange, and who spoke with broad Cumbrian accents and curious forms of expression like the long drawn out 'Eeehh' with which they would initiate their frequent exclamations of wonder and surprise.

My mother's Uncle Ned, was a tailor. My mother remembers seeing him in his workshop sitting cross-legged, sewing. In about 1928, when my mother was eight, he died. He was aged around fifty, and probably died of pneumonia. The stability that my mother had known for several years thus came to an end, and she had to go back to live with her father, and those of her brothers and sisters who had not already left home, and who had come back from their own foster families: 'they were like strangers to me', she has said.

Her father in the meantime had remarried, a younger woman, with whom he went on to have three more children. She was not in the same mould as my grandmother, who by all accounts was a loving, gentle woman, full of life and laughter. Perhaps marrying an older man, inheriting his large family, and being responsible for managing the household on a railway clerk's wage would try anyone's humanity. My own mother and her stepmother did not take to each other, and my mother maintains a cold view of her stepmother on account of the hard time she had with her, and the beatings she received from her.

The family moved to Whitby, where they ran a guest house to supplement the railway wage, and then later to the nearby village of Aislaby, where they ran the New Inn. My mother has described how she would sometimes have to serve the men in the bar with their pints of beer, while they played dominoes, and talked. (When my Auntie Dot died in the nineties, she was buried in the churchyard at Aislaby and the funeral meal was held in the same New Inn. One of my cousin's children was working there.)

My mother, like most of her siblings, was academically bright, and won, a year early, a scholarship to Whitby Grammar School. Despite her ability and thirst for learning (which remains to this day), her experience there was mainly unhappy. Her memories are of bullying, sarcastic teachers, and the gulf that existed between her own straitened family circumstances (always the anxieties around not having the right uniform, or the right books, or the right games kit) and those of the relatively well-off fee-paying majority.

'I left as soon as I could,' she says. 'I left at fifteen, even though I wasn't meant to leave the Grammar School till I was sixteen. I just said I'm not going back.' She got a job in a shop at Sandsend, a traditional grocer's, where she served customers, and bagged up the sugar. The situation at home with her stepmother not being any easier, she was looking for ways to get out of that too. A family friend had an idea, and helped her apply to become a nurse in a sanatorium, for TB patients, because it was one of the few places that would take you on at sixteen, and provide board and lodging. And that is the tender age at which she left home for the outside world, in this case in the country near Worksop, and, as she says, 'I've kept myself ever since.'

As I contemplate my mother's story, I realise how much detail I know about her life, and how little I know about my father's. As I grew older I was able to question her on the details, and take in her fund of stories, and relate the different parts to each other to make a comprehensible chronology in my own mind. With my father I never had the chance, and there have been no living relatives to question. I remember once, while he was in his wheelchair, asking him if he'd had dealings with the Japs in the war. (I was an avid reader of Wizard and Tiger and other comics, which had numerous graphically illustrated stories of battles with the Jerries or the Japs or the Nips.) I remember him smiling at me and telling me stuff, but I cannot remember what it was: I was too young to understand or take in the detail at one telling. It needs repeat versions of that kind of oral history to get the whole story, and I never got the chance. From what I have been able to piece together since, he was out in the Far East on a destroyer, towards the end of the war, having made an epic voyage out there from Britain in a small flotilla of Motor Launches. There are photos of captured Japanese soldiers against a background of tropical islands, and some souvenirs - a Japanese compass and watch, no doubt liberated from said prisoners.

I come to the end of the stretch of river that I am following, and after crossing the River Derwent where it enters the Ouse, my route takes me through Barmby on the Marsh. Barmby is at the end of a four mile long road from Howden, the next major settlement, and the end of the line for motor cars. I have been able to approach Barmby from the west, a privilege denied to motor vehicles. In an isolated situation like this, Barmby might feel like an abandoned and neglected medieval relic, but in truth it somehow still has the indefinable air of a living community.

I take some time out to wander along a back lane and am rewarded with sight of a curious brick-built farm building, two storeyed, with the ground floor open to the elements via three brick arches on each side. I ponder its purpose, but fail to come to a conclusion. At the nearby church, I bump into a small group of village ladies about to go in and no doubt do their traditional clean up and tidy job. Round the corner of the church, I see old grave stones haphazardly leaning amongst rough grass, while the six Drax towers do their cooling in the background.

Dances, dances, dances

I set off on the few miles to Howden, looking forward perhaps to a touch of relatively sophisticated civilisation, including possibly a smidgeon of café society – hope springs eternal.

While my father spent most of the war years in motor launches in coastal waters, and then a couple of years based in what is now The Gambia, and then in the Far East, my mother spent most of them in Helmsley, a small market town at the south west edge of the North Yorkshire Moors. Nursing had served its purpose and come to an end, and her father had suggested she apply to work for the railways. So she ended up in Helmsley working in the booking office as part of a small team of young women replacing men gone to the war. She lived in digs across the road from the station with a Miss Sunley (as a child, I had rather boring visits to her house too). She shared the digs with Kath, who remained a friend till the end of her life (as a child, we stayed with Kath and her family). The other important person in their group was Betty, a local lass who later with husband Don ran a successful market garden and green grocery business in the town. When I was a child we went and stayed with Don and Betty several times too.

The main focus of life for these young women (my mother would have been nineteen when the war started) seems to have been a full-on social life greatly facilitated by the setting up of a large army camp in nearby Duncombe Park, a local estate. Dances, dances, and more dances seem to have been the order of the day, and with the imbalance in the gender numbers it was no doubt heady stuff for young women to find themselves very much in demand. Amongst my mother's photos is a great bundle showing a series of young men in various service uniforms, some of them darkly handsome Poles. It seems to have been the custom for admirers to hand over a portrait of themselves, perhaps hoping to cement a bond, or perhaps hoping to improve their chances of being remembered amongst so many others. I'm not sure if my mother reciprocated, and whether there are, scattered across the country in the photograph collections of now elderly men, portraits of an attractive young woman with a flashing smile and laughing eyes. I suspect not. She gives the impression of very determinedly not settling down to anything very serious, but instead enjoying a gay and exciting time.

"We'd have been out to a dance the night before, and got in late, and Miss Sunley would be calling me telling me it was time to get up or I'd be late for work. I'd get up just in time to flee across the road and get into the booking office in time for the first train to be puffing in. The old station master would make remarks and complain and say 'Where've you been?' and I'd just say 'In bed!' "

'When the trains came in, sometimes there'd be hundreds of soldiers arriving or coming back from leave. We had to collect the tickets and were supposed to check them, but there were so many in the crush that you couldn't do it. Some of them would shove old bus tickets or bits of paper in your hand and they'd all go past grinning and joking.

'One time they got the military police from the camp to come and check tickets, but they had to hold everyone up for so long to do it that they never bothered again.'

Sometime after the war, my mother heard from her brother Jim, at that point living in Hull with his wife Dot, and their two young children. Dot was unwell. My mother moved to Hull in order, as I understand it, to be near them and be able to offer help and support. Perhaps life in Helmsley without the army camp was beginning to pall and the lights of the relatively big city were beginning to exert their pull. Perhaps with men back from the war there was a push for women to give up their wartime railway jobs. My mother lodged with Dot and Jim in Hull, and got a clerical job of some kind.

Oddly vulnerable

Howden is picturesque and unusual. Its middle is dominated by a spectacular, large, ancient, and partially ruined Minster church. Also in the middle is an area of green space dominated by moated fish ponds. I return to them later, but in the meantime I wander round exploring. I find something peculiarly satisfying about approaching a strange town at the pace, and with the advantages, that a bicycle affords. I don't have to worry about finding somewhere to park. I have time to take in my surroundings and get my bearings, and if I'm feeling rushed I simply pull into the side to give myself time – without incurring the wrath and indignation of fellow motorists honking and cursing and trying to squeeze past on a narrow roadway. I'm coming in at a human pace, as people would have done for the first couple of thousand years of the settlement's existence. Places were meant to be approached in human terms, because human terms were the only terms there were. Modern places which are designed to be approached by motorised transport are inhuman and therefore usually uniformly ghastly.

I lock my bike to the Minster railings and go in. I'm not really in the mood for church interiors however, and soon come out. I spot a couple of cafes, but I'm convinced they flatter to deceive, especially for someone of my narrow dietary tastes, so I don't go in.

I see a large office belonging to the Press Association, and don't understand what it's doing in this very pleasant but remote neck of the woods. I assume it's some kind of token head office left over up here for some historical reason but later I discover that it is a serious place of business, staffed by lots of reporters providing agency reports for newspapers nationally and beyond.

I see also an appealing green grocer's, in which I buy apples, and tomatoes, and – a particular favourite – cashew nuts. I head for the moated fish ponds, where I sit on a bench and consume some of the recently acquired food, and contemplate my surroundings. I forego the opportunity to read the interpretation boards I can see nearby. Moated fish ponds are probably medieval, and maybe monastic, and knowing what their history is doesn't at this moment feel like it will add to my enjoyment. Maybe there's a lesson there for me on my quest into the history of myself and my family. If I find out more will it really add to my pleasure and enjoyment, I ask myself. Yes, comes back the answer at once. Of course it will. There's no comparison between moated fish ponds, medieval or not, and your own origins. Get real.

And thus admonished, I gather the remnants of my cashew nuts and apples together, and leave Howden, heading south-east.

Over the M62 I have a choice of routes and decide to go with the longer one in order to maximise time on the riverbank. It may be a riverbank but any resemblance to the tales of Ratty and friends ends there. The river manifests here as a broad lake. And then the riverbank becomes a short industrial portscape. This latter is in the shape of a place called Hook, an outlier for Goole, on the opposite bank. My route turns away from the river here to cut across the neck of an extravagant meander and exchange five miles of river route for one mile of road. The last scene of this shortcut takes place in extraordinary parkland. Flat land, undivided by fences or field boundaries stretches all around. Mature trees, some with their dark green foliage right down to the ground, stand alone at intervals. The horizon, in the middle distance is composed of more trees. The land is covered in a crop that I cannot name, but seems to be a species of grass or herb. It is about eighteen inches high, has now come to maturity and is creating a brown rust coloured sea all around. The road meanders as a single strip of dark tarmac between the rusty ground and the silent trees. All is still, and no other human or creature is about as I wend my way through this peaceful strange landscape. Only two dead squirrels lying at the edge of the road keep me any kind of company. One is lying on its side, and the other is sprawled on its back with its mouth open, looking oddly vulnerable, and very dead. Towards the end of the parkland, a line of mature horse chestnuts display their customary early sensitivity to encroaching autumn by turning from green to orange and yellow.

Emerging once more at the river, although all sign of it is hidden behind the giant levee rearing above my head, I bump into an old guy on the other side of the road. He's wearing walking boots and using a couple of ski type walking sticks. He hails me to ask if I've seen a party of walkers anywhere, and I say no, and stop to see if I can help him find his people, and also chat, which I suspect is his main interest. I guess he's in his seventies, wearing a flat cap, and with a southern, maybe London accent. I try to work out where his party is or might be, with the aid of my map (he doesn't have one), but he's a bit vague about it all. He should have met up with the party this morning, but was late, and they'd already set off when he got to the rendezvous. He's not even sure whether they were heading upstream or down, so he could be going in completely the wrong direction. None of this seems to really worry him. He tells me he's got a dicky knee, and he's recovering from a recent heart attack.

"What I like to do," he says, "is wander along and stop and look at anything that interests me. I'm curious. I look at the scenery, at the path, at the view. If there's a BT notice on a pole, I like to stop and read it, find out what they're up to. This group I'm a member of - we get together and go for walks of five miles or eight or fifteen. Of course, I can't do the long ones, I just go as far as I can, and then turn round. These others – they like to get their heads down and keep going, talking all the time, not noticing what's around. They're always having to wait for me to catch up." He laughs a little. "I might be being a bit paranoid, but I suspect they might have set off quite promptly this morning when I was late, not too disappointed that I wasn't there."

I laugh at this, and at the other little self-deprecating jokes that he sprays around in his conversation. I notice the bags under his eyes, and the slight anxious look on his face. Getting older, his health deteriorating, perhaps living alone with his wife gone and children grown up and far away (he makes no mention of family), he has a right to be a little diffident in the face of an uncertain future. I admire his continuing interest in life, and the way he forges a good-humoured present for himself despite the difficulties. I notice also that he is of an age to be my father, and feel I notice an undercurrent of fatherliness in his dealings with me: the assumption of a ready intimacy, the jokiness, the enthusiasm. I, in my turn, notice an undercurrent of filial feeling in our encounter: a pleasure in his company and anything he says because he says it, a concern for his welfare and safety, and a sensitivity to his need to maintain his independence as long as possible. Like the squirrel on its back, he too seems oddly vulnerable, but, as yet, not dead.

We bring our meeting to an end via a shared enthusiasm for the value of maps. He tells me that he heard a recent radio programme comparing our own British maps to those on the continent, and that ours, with their wealth of detail, are streets (or contours, perhaps) ahead. He heads upstream in, I assume, vain pursuit of his party. I head a little further downstream, where I spot some steps climbing the levee, and unable to resist so clear an invitation, take myself up to the top.

Lift and carry

The top of the levee here is close mowed like a lawn, and there are two or three benches available to rest upon, and so I sit down. In front of me I see a strip of land shelving down to the water's edge covered in tall grasses and wild plants. Beyond that is a wild expanse of water, long lines of froth on its surface, and almost choppy under the influence of the stiff breeze that has got up. I look closely and decide that the tide is not only coming in, but is well up. A piece of blackened wood that I can see is slowly moving upstream. The far bank is indeed very far away, and the low territory beyond not much visible. Behind me is the narrow strip of the road running here parallel to the levee, and on the other side a short row of houses, their first floors a little below the level at which I am sitting. One is for sale. How would an estate agent blurb handle this situation? Instructions to seller showing buyers round: whatever you do don't mention the flooding...

Setting off, I move away from the river again and dreamily cross the flat lands of this strange region. For an hour and more I drift contentedly across an empty landscape, seeing only one car in that time. The day is grey, but I am happy enough, my legs turning easily, and the breeze behind me. Ploughed or harrowed fields with hardly a fence in sight extend on each side of my narrow strip of tarmacked road. Field boundaries are mostly marked by neat ditches, with water running idly in the bottoms. Occasional larger drainage canals are crossed by bridges. At the exit from one tiny village, two rows of Lombardy poplars on each side of the road bring a flavour of French countryside to this East Yorkshire scene. These fields, that in medieval and later times would have been busy with gangs of labourers working the land, are empty now. The mechanisation of agriculture means, I suspect that most of this land surface is now untouched by human foot.

My own family connections with the land are not far below the surface (so to speak). It is not so long ago that the majority of people earned their living from the land, so there is nothing particularly unusual in having an earthy connection. Of the twelve of my mother's male ancestors that I have been able to track down, half of them were farmers, or nurserymen, or husbandmen. Of fifteen on my dad's side however, six of them were mariners or fishermen. Agriculture and the sea, two major resources before industry came along.

My mother's sister married a farmer and they had the small farm on the moors near Whitby where I went to stay a lot as a child. My dad and mum had gone to stay there with us when we were little children, before the accident. I have a rare early memory of my dad here: doing some building work with my uncle Bede on one of the cowsheds. They were chiselling some of the concrete off the end of the low platform on which the cattle were tethered for milking. My dad, like a lot of naval men, seems to have been very practical, and able to turn his hand to most jobs. I know from the way he has talked that my uncle liked my dad, and that they got on well together. In fact everyone who has ever spoken of my dad has liked him, and spoken warmly about him.

So it must have been hard for them when this man that they knew and liked was rendered so incapable by his accident. I recall a visit that we made to the farm. We had a little Morris Minor, (which I think came via some government transport support scheme for disabled people) with a soft top that could be pulled back in order that we could hoist dad into the car. My uncle Jim, who could drive from his days in the army but didn't own a car, took a few driving lessons so he could bring his skills up to date, and drive us about. The idea was that we could take dad out on trips. I'm not sure how often we actually did this – I remember only a few occasions, but there may have been more. I would imagine it was a lot of effort for I'm not sure how much actual pleasure. On this occasion we made the journey from Leeds to near Whitby, which probably took us a couple of hours. Dad was in the front, and mum, my brother and I in the back. When we got there, we didn't have the hoist, or I think the wheelchair, with us, as there wasn't room. Usually on trips out, when we got somewhere therefore, dad just sat in the car till it was time to go home again, while the rest of us might sit nearby, or we children would play nearby.

But as I stood by the car on the hard, sun dried mud outside the range of stone farm buildings and watched and listened, the plan this time seemed to be to get dad inside, and sit him in a chair in the house. This meant lifting him and carrying him. Of course Bede and one of his sons, probably Tony, were practical men, used to carrying and managing all sorts of loads, including live ones, like sheep, or calves. They worked out how they'd do it, in conjunction with dad: a discussion about how to best do the job such as they would have had at other times in the past.

My dad had grown heavier through his enforced inactivity, and was a significant weight to carry. Just prior to the lift, I remember him giving some final words of warning, delivered with a kind of level cheerfulness:

'Sometimes my body goes into a kind of spasm, and jerks suddenly. Don't worry about it, I can't feel anything and I'm not in pain. Just carry on.'

And they did, lifting him between them using their linked hands and arms as a cradle to hold him in, and carrying him inside.

Welcome You

'Faxfleet Welcome You,' says the sign outside the hamlet, whose inhabitants either enjoy idiosyncratic grammar, or consider themselves a true community, and think of themselves and their settlement always as a 'we', and never as an 'it'.

Just prior to coming to Faxfleet, a rise in the road over a major drainage channel entering the river had revealed the tide well up and the water flooding up to some kind of valve lock system under the road. On the landward side, the level of the water was right down in the drain, several feet below the river level, and this low level of water disappeared inland in a straight line between its own, smaller-scale levees. There was something mysterious, almost magical, about this intertidal drainage control system operating so effectively on its own. Although perhaps the folk that maintain it would demur about the 'on its own' bit.

From a car-park at the end of the settlement, I make my way to the top of the levee, and look out over an area of wetlands to the river. Beyond that is yet more flat land, and then, seemingly in the middle of fields, a ship progressing steadily inland. Realising it must be on a different branch of the river, I enjoy the incongruity of the sight. Then, the connection being ships, I wonder again, as I've wondered before, about my dad's war service. What effect did it have on him? Plenty of men came home from the war with bad experiences bottled up inside, and left it to their families, especially wives, to take the strain. Maybe my dad's sensible, down-to-earth cheerfulness took him through all the difficulties. Maybe he had a 'lucky' war with boredom and inaction the main features.

My reveries are interrupted by a meeting with the driver of a wagon which is parked below and who has come up to admire the scenery.

'I don't often drive up this way to deliver,' he says. 'I've just delivered to a farm we don't normally go to. I don't usually come this side of the Humber. Thought I'd just come up here and have a look. Ah. Wetlands.'

We discuss the view, and the ship, and going down to the Humber Bridge. I discuss with him my thoughts on levees and the houses that exist in the shadow of these great banks, and the flood risk they therefore live with. We both, rather unkindly, seem to find this amusing, and share a laugh together.

He's probably in his forties, interested in what's about him. 'Hm,' he says, looking again at the view, 'I think I'll bring some binoculars with me next time, keep them in the wagon.'

We remark on the wind, which is getting up. He tells me about his wagon. 'If you've got a few tons on, and the wind's against you on the motorway, there's no way you can get into top gear with that old thing,' he says without rancour. 'It's getting on a bit now.'

He's been keen to share a moment with someone else in the solitary ordinariness of his day, but the time comes to move on, and we go back down to the car park. He rumbles off inland. I head along a track with the bank of the levee on my right, and the great river, unseen now, flowing silently behind it.

Of love and words

At Weighton Lock, an extremely large construction that controls the junction between the Market Weighton canal and the River Humber, a stone plaque commemorates the efforts of some of the men who constructed it in 1775. Or at least commemorates some of the men who organised those other men who actually constructed it: Mr Grundy, Engineer; Mr Allen, Surveyor; Mr Jefferson, Mason; and my particular favourite, because he is the representative of a trade not normally recognised, Mr Smith, Carpenter.

Shortly after crossing the lock, my track heads away from the river bank, and slants off inland. I enter the road system again at a little place called Broomfleet, which I characterise to myself as unpretentious, and unspoiled by modern buildings. Leyland cypress, an alien weed which is colonising our fair land is, however, here, and trying to spoil everything, as it tries to do almost everywhere. The odd thing about this unfortunate tree is that it spreads, not by accidental growth, but through being deliberately planted by people paying out good money to buy bad plants.

A van outside a house announces 'Recumbent Bicycles' on its side, and then coming towards me I see an extremely bright single headlight, followed closely by one of the said recumbent bicycles. I am so impressed by this superior version of bicycling style, that, rather than waving, I find myself saluting the man lounging back as he propels himself through the world. 'Good morning!' he calls. 'Good morning!' I call back, though by rights it should be 'Good Morning, Sir.'

Just as I'm about to leave Broomfleet, I find a bench beneath a tree on a little green, and, recognising cyclists' perfection at once, I stop for a break and a feed. While I am so engaged, another fellow cyclist, on a conventional machine this time, passes me, pauses, and we greet each other. He is also a tourist, with panniers, following the trans-Pennine trail, which here coincides with my own route. 'How far is it to Hessle? he enquires, and I reply that it is about twelve miles. He heads off, and I continue to eat. I contemplate the next stage, and then beyond that to my night's lodging. I have not booked again. Will I get to Hull and go through my usual number: angst-ridden incompetence, riding the innumerable gutters of the city whilst visualising sleeping in them? Almost certainly yes, but in the meantime I describe it in a more positive light. I will, I say to myself, feel my way in, and see what happens.

Only a few miles further on, I start to recognise the signs of industrial civilisation once more. There are commercial premises. There are vehicles passing me. There is the sound of roaring traffic ahead. My long journey across the empty flatlands of rural East Yorkshire is drawing to a close, and I'm not sure when I will see their like again; or where I shall sleep tonight. My positivity on accommodation has worn thin already, and a mood of faint depression hangs around me in its usual slovenly fashion. At a small village called Ellerker I have the inconvenience of an uphill gradient to deal with, something I have not exerted myself on for a day and a half. More and bigger hills, the edge of the Wolds as I take them to be, have been growing larger before my eyes for the last hour or so. Now, it appears, their outliers have claimed me. No doubt there is worse to come.

What with the faint depression and the uphill, I take to practicing being aware of my breathing. This often helps. I remind myself that Thich Nhat Hanh says if you breathe with awareness three times, you can come back to yourself. He has some good things to say on love too. In his tradition of Buddhism at least, it's not considered possible to love anyone else, or do good in the world, unless you yourself feel sufficiently loved. And if there's no-one else around to love you, you better just get down to it and do it yourself. This runs counter to our more puritan western ethos, where self-sacrifice and others-before-self are more highly regarded as expressions of love. Self-love fits more easily with new age style thinking, though I think new age has a tendency towards narcissistic self-sufficiency, rather than the interpersonal communion that Buddhism (or at least some traditions of it) recommends. So, overcoming and ignoring my puritan scruples, and flirting with the dangers of new age narcissism, I incorporate some self-love into my breathing awareness: 'breathing in, I know I am loving myself; breathing out, I know I am loving myself.' I find it soothing, and calming.

Suddenly, on the outskirts of Ellerker, near a garage by a small crossroads, and with the sound of traffic in the distance, I have the realisation that my dad loved me. Of course he loved me. My mother has told me he did. But previously I seemed to know he loved me just as words in the air. Now I feel the reality of it in a new way. I feel myself as him, loving his small child, me, with all his being. I feel the preciousness of my small being to him. I feel how much of his energy and thought and care were bound up in me, and later in my brother. I know how much I loved my children when they were small, not as a theoretical construct or as a warm glow, but as a visceral imperative wrapped up in their bodies, and their actions, and their safety, and the minute to minute, day to day needs of their happiness. I suddenly know that that is how he loved me too. How could it be otherwise – I am his son; I learned love from him, and from my mother. I had that experience in my body for six years when he could hold me, and look after me, and be part of me. And I had it for a further three years when he could look at me and talk to me, and smile at me.

Of course I'm starting to cry as I realise these things, and I lean my bike against the back of the Ellerker sign, and turn a little away from the road to hide myself. My dad really loved me. Of course he did. Of course he did. It's big; it's a good realisation to have. That's how it is, that's how I see it now.

I look around from my stance behind the sign, and see an ordinary little crossroads, with a garage nearby. Across the way, my road leads on ahead.

Join the navy

After crossing a noisy dual carriageway via a bridge, I pass through the village of Brantingham. Feeling stiff, I stand up on the pedals to ease my various muscles and joints into slightly different positions. Guiding the bike via my fingertips on the handlebars, I hold the position and enjoy the delicate sense of poise and balance as I glide along the road.

As a child, I studied the photographs of my father doing his gymnastic work. There are pictures of him, dressed immaculately in his naval PT kit, stretched out and holding positions against the bars in the gym. His muscles stand out, and he looks incredibly fit and well. After he was gone, I wanted to know whatever I could find out about him. The photos were one of my sources of that information. I wanted, like most sons at that age, to be like him. I wanted to follow him; I wanted him to lead me. My mother once asked me what I wanted to do when I grew up. It was when I was still at primary school, maybe a year or so after he died. I told her I thought I might go into the navy. 'Oh no,' she said, 'oh no.'

Her discouragement, worried and unhurried, had a strong effect on me, and I remember it vividly. In the end, I didn't go into the navy. Probably I wouldn't have done so anyway, whatever her response. I was having the dreams of a ten year old, and my older, adolescent self headed towards different aims and goals.

I have often wondered about this incident. She was probably, like many mothers, ambitious for me, in the sense of wanting me to fulfil my potential. She wouldn't see the navy, or at least my father's route through it, as offering me that fulfilment. Possibly she was reluctant to see her son risk the same end as his father, and who could blame her for that? But what I was after, I realise now, was not a realistic career guidance session. I would have liked, in a perfect world, a simple acknowledgement that my dad must be important to me, and that it was perfectly natural, at my age, to want to follow in his footsteps. It could have been coupled with a brief, smiling reminder that people change over time, and that as I got older, I'd probably find different things I wanted to do. (After all, I'd already been through several stages, including sheep farmer in Australia.) My mother, grieving and suffering herself, did the best she could in the circumstances. Maybe the person who could have best communicated this message to me was my dad, and he of course, was dead.

My route recrosses the dual carriageway over another bridge, and then turns to run parallel to it. It is an unpleasant experience, with thunderous traffic crashing past me only a few yards away on the other side of a narrow fenced off verge, where a few trees and shrubs suffer this madness all the time. Beyond the traffic, a wooded escarpment slope also runs parallel to my route, but I am less in the mood to admire it, and more in the mood to hurry on and see if I can find peace away from the franticness.

But peace does not come easy. I find myself following some cycle route signs that have appeared, and trusting them rather than my map I make fast progress, but am not really clear where I am going. Sometimes that's OK ('let's just go with the flow here folks...'), but on this occasion, coupled with anxiety that is surfacing about entering the big city, and where I rest my weary head tonight, I start to enter into hot and bothered territory. The signs take me down off the road, past a large school (shiver of unpleasant associations) towards the dual carriageway again. I lose my faith in these signs, and, after humming and hawing, and looking at the map, I turn back on myself. I follow instead a series of dots on the map that is meant to take me on a local cycle route into Hull via minor roads. This is good. What is not good is that the first section of this minor route is a long haul uphill. The road is also a busy road, and I walk slowly, pushing my burden, passed by rushing vehicles. I examine, as I pass it close by, the details of a very large stone quarry, the series of machines working there, and the clouds of dust that they create. Eventually leaving the quarry and traffic behind as I turn off on to a truly minor road, I still continue to haul myself up steep gradients. I am convinced I have made an error in coming on this route, and I am giving myself a hard time internally, as well as suffering a little on the outside.

As the gradient slackens off towards the top, I find a gradual return to a sense of balance. My irritation and my botheredness start to melt away. I remember that journeys have their own momentum, and that the route I have taken may not be the biggest mistake in the world, but may turn out to be exactly right. I remember to breathe, and it helps. Just beyond a sign saying Swanland ('Twinned with Lestrem, France') I stop by a bench. I have my own personal litter bin right next to me. I rest. I eat. I put my rubbish in the bin. I look around. Near me, on the summit of the hill is a large water tower. From this distance it looks like a wedding cake on legs: round, flat-topped and covered all over in frothy white icing.

Closer to, it reveals itself as an almost elegant construction, the twelve white legs on which it stands joined together at their tops by arches. Neat gravel paths behind an ironwork gate set it off nicely and a door in its central pillar with a window above add a touch of mystery (what for...? where to...?). The date of its construction – 1931 – is displayed proudly, alongside a coat of arms with three crowns on. They really don't build them like that anymore.

I suddenly get a strong sense of my dad's presence. I remember a photograph of him in his back yard, aged about ten, proudly holding a bicycle. He could have cycled up here. We're now on the outskirts of Hull. I'm on his home turf. It's as though we could be here together now, and he, an old man now, is exclaiming excitedly, 'I remember this, I used to come and see this when I was a lad. We used to get on our bikes and race up here to see it.'

Built when he was ten, it would have been a landmark worth visiting over the next two or three years. I'm excited to realise I'm now in his territory. Just as I roamed around the Leeds area, he could have roamed around this area. The thirties would have been a great time for cycling because the traffic volumes would have been minimal compared to today. I try to minimise my own golden-age romantic tendencies, but surely here is a perfect example of where the past was much better than the present. What did he actually do, how far did he get, back then? He can't answer for himself, so I have to answer for him.

'We had a great time. I had a bike, and so did some of my friends and we used to cycle all over in the summer. We'd go off for the day with our lunches and explore for miles. I always liked seeing new places.'

'I'm like you, dad. I like exploring on a bike. Isn't that funny? I've got a really good memory for routes. I can always remember when I've cycled somewhere before.'

'There's always something different to see, and talk about. It was safe back then – hardly any traffic you see. I had such a tremendous sense of freedom from riding around and exploring. I sometimes wonder if that's why I joined the navy.'

'So you joined the navy to see the world?'

We both laugh.

'Yeah, and you know what I saw?'

'You saw the sea!'

And we both laugh again.

Clan territory

Swanland, when I arrive down the hill into it, has a pond in the middle. Perhaps this is where the swans lived. Further on I pass a couple of schools and cross a main road. It's busy – school run time no doubt, and I am passed by traffic that sometimes gets too close, and in my view is being careless with my safety for the sake of a few seconds saved on their (probably unnecessary) journey. Not unnaturally I get peeved. I try and remain calm and philosophical as usual, and concentrate on defensive cycling. Instead I actually get something very different. I get angry, with a deeply primitive sense of territoriality strongly bound up in it.

'This is my home, this is my dad's place. I have a right to be here through him, and you should show more respect. Especially if, as I suspect, you're newcomers. If so, you have less right to be here than me. Watch out, or I'll get him and his mates to sort you out.'

As a child I never felt the security of family or clan support allied to territory. I missed that sense of protection that a father can bring. From when I was six he was paralysed, and he could not physically protect me or sort things out. In fact I felt the need to protect him in his vulnerable physical state. We were living in places that were alien to him as well as to me. When I was nine, he died, and was gone, and I was left to manage as best as I could. I couldn't then say 'My dad will sort this out.' I couldn't say it to others as a warning or a threat. And I couldn't say it to myself as a comfort. I didn't feel I had proper protection. I was left thin-skinned and vulnerable. I feel I never properly developed the tough, useful, permeable boundaries that should have been my heritage, that come with a sense of security from father and family and healthy menfolk. Instead my edges, sometimes disguised behind a façade of bravado, always seemed fragile and brittle, and likely to fracture and fragment under stress.

From my current height I get a view of what looks like the whole of Hull spread out below me, and then it's downhill and into the city. I see my first Hull telephone box; it's white, and it does look alien. Otherwise, the suburbia seems very comparable to suburbia everywhere: nondescript. I pass through Hessle, the first urban centre, with shops and ancient churches. Because it is very busy, and I have to avoid broken glass in the gutter, and it's very hard to work out my route on the ground compared to the map, then I'm afraid that the clichéd non-joke that I've been manfully resisting for a long time works its way up into my conscious mind and sits there smugly triumphant: Hessle is a hassle.

Coming out of Hessle, I find myself on a type of dual carriageway, one of those built as part of a large, possibly pre-war, housing development when land use was less of an issue and they were more generous with space than is feasible today. Between the carriageways is a grass verge, profusely covered in trees and shrubs. There is little traffic on the road, and such as there is has been shepherded into the outside lane. The inside part of the inside lane has been designated a cycle lane, and the outer part has been painted with white cross-hatching to provide a four or five foot safety margin between we cyclists and the traffic. I give a mental three cheers for the good burghers of Hull, or at least for their cycling officer, for creating this little haven. I hope there is more to come. Unfortunately, some of the good people of Hull do not value their cycle lane as I do, and have parked their vehicles squarely across it, forcing me to veer out into the traffic. A plague on your houses, I say.

My route to the heart of the city takes me, as a cyclist, through some of the less appealing parts of the urban sprawl. Shuttered shops, struggling people, back streets and boarded up houses pass me by alongside new city centre estates and tower blocks that my dad would not have recognised. I keep wondering whether he might have been along streets I am now traversing, whether what I am seeing were familiar sights to him. I particularly like, amongst a network of terraced streets, an old police station, brick built, with freshly painted blue doors and window frames. Would he have known this as a boy? Would this place have been an object of fear and fascination for him and his friends?

I get lost amongst the new developments and back streets and ask an old guy where the city centre is. He points me in a certain direction and tells me it's a couple of minutes away. His accent sounds a bit like the Leeds accent to me.

I cycle on to major roads, and amongst large institutions like department stores, railway stations and civic buildings. There is no escaping the fact, and I have to face it square on: I am now into finding-a-bed-for-the-night territory. Remembering my Selbyville horror story, I decide to go straight for the jugular. My internet researches before I left have provided me with the addresses and telephone numbers of some possible establishments. One is a large city centre hotel, recently refurbished, which advertised rooms from £40 per night. I am willing to fork out on this extravagance in return for bypassing the trudging the streets bit of my normal method. I locate it close to the station and, locking my bike to its railings, enter its portals before I have a chance to bethink myself. The extensive lobby is crowded with comings and goings, customers and staff, luggage and noise. I am mercifully anonymous whilst I study the set-up. Close to the check-in desk is a tariff board. I saunter over to read it. My perusal reveals that a single room here goes at the rate of £140 per night. Hmm. Inflation in Hull city centre hotels seems to be a little above the national average. I saunter out of the hotel, and back to the streets.

I cycle a little out of the city centre and investigate a motel, but don't like the look of it. I cycle on, amongst the noise and busyness and anonymity of the alien city centre traffic. I am getting close to the familiar feeling of desperate gutter searching, but with last night's painful experience to remind me, I at least know that that is what I am doing. This makes it more painful: the pain of wandering around lost and helpless, and the added pain of knowing that I'm being a pathetic idiot. Something finally breaks and I do a sensible thing: I get my phone out and call one of the numbers on my list.

A teenager answers, and in answer to my enquiry, tells me she's sorry but they are full. I am, sensibly, looking at the next number on my list, when, to my surprise, my phone rings. There is a woman's voice on the other end asking me if I've just rung asking about a room. It is the teenager's mother saying her daughter doesn't know what she's talking about, and there is a room for the night for me. I am relieved and happy and impressed to be rung back so swiftly. I head up the road, or as I've discovered they say round here, 'rerd'. There are a couple of miles to go to find relative safety.

Hidden story

After we've sorted out details like where to put my bike and the time of breakfast, I chat with the landlady as she shows me my room, which is on the first floor at the front. The other people staying seem to be mostly builders. She also tells me she sometimes gets parents staying who are visiting their offspring at the Uni down the road. After a little while she asks me directly, 'So what are you doing in Hull?' There is a faint emphasis on the 'you' which seems to me to say, 'People on bicycles are normally on holiday. People on holiday don't normally come to Hull.'

I tell her a little about my cycle ride across the country and about visiting places that are connected with my own history. I tell her about the visit to the house in Leeds. I tell her that my dad grew up in Hull, and that I'd had the thought that as a boy he may have cycled up to Swanland, which I have just come through. Perhaps it is this first use in Hull of my family connection, perhaps this assertion of my connectedness with the place, that leads to a greater confidence between us, but an interesting story emerges.

We have been discussing the yearning that people have to find out more about their family, about how important it is to them to know something about their roots. She tells me that she has recently discovered a fabrication at the heart of her own family history.

'We'd always understood that my mother's mother, my grandmother, died when my mother was a baby. But when we buried my grandfather recently I noticed that the dates for her death, which were on the gravestone at the family plot, were wrong. They had her death down as much more recent – when my mother would have been a teenager, or young adult. I did some asking around and I found out that my grandmother was not dead while my mother was growing up, but was in a mental institution. She'd been committed while my mother was a baby, and the family had decided to cover it up with the fiction of her death. There are younger members of my family who still don't know the truth.'

We discuss the stigma around mental illness that makes people consider going to such lengths. The way in which the shame surrounding the original committal is compounded by the shame and distress of having to keep the whole thing secret.

'I wonder what it must have done to your mother to have had to keep that story hidden,' I ask.

'My mother had her own mental health problems,' she tells me. 'She was committed several times. She had three children in under three years, and then her husband left, and she was struggling. In the street where we lived people knew she was a bit on the edge. I remember as a child seeing this girl from down the street goading my mother. She goaded her, and goaded her, till my mother snapped and tried to hit her. She didn't manage to do it, but the police were still called and, of course, because she had the reputation, she was sectioned and carted off.'

We discuss whether the stigma around mental illness is less now than it was. We decide it is less, but that shame still surrounds the whole area.

The landlady is still curious about my family and asks more details about my father's story. I tell her about the navy, and where he'd served in the war. I tell her about the accident in Portsmouth, and his death later. I tell her that his parents, who also lived in Hull, are both dead, as is his only brother. His brother's only child, my cousin, is the only relative I'm aware of who may still be alive, but we'd lost contact with her about forty years ago, so the trail is very cold. She may have left Hull for example. I say I'd been wondering whether a letter to a local paper might help to track her down, or maybe even find people who knew my dad. It seems a long shot.

The conversation in this neat anonymous room in the suburbs of Hull peters to a close. She has to get on with being a landlady, and I have to go out again if I want to do any more exploring before it gets dark.

In the vanguard

I cycle along near the University, which at this time in the evening is undergoing something of a rush hour. I am looking for Chanterlands Avenue. My grandparents lived in a house in Aisne Street, but my internet researches have failed to discover it, so I assume it may have been demolished. However, I know it was near, or off, Chanterlands Avenue, so I'm thinking I may at least get a sense of the area. I find Chanterlands, which is a long, busy, through route, with a cemetery down the bottom end. There are areas of terraced houses similar to what Aisne Street must have been like: I have seen photos of the front of the house.

Feeling I have done as much as can be done for the time being, I head off towards the city centre. I pass a newsagent in the process of shutting up shop for the evening. It is now dusk and the volume of traffic has decreased as people have no doubt got to their homes and their teas by the fire. On a whim I do the thing that, if I had been sensible, I would have done before: I go in and buy a street map of Hull. Standing in the street outside the shop by my bike, I open up the map and look at the index. And what do you know? Aisne Street is there. And it is just off Chanterlands, at the bottom end. So much for internet searches.

I get back on the bike, and hurry round to Aisne Street. It's a small road of terraced houses hidden away in a little network of five streets that form a self-contained unit: you go into them, and you come out again, and you can't get through to anywhere else. There are thirty-seven houses in Aisne Street, and I don't know which the relevant one is. I haven't brought the scrap of paper with me on which I'd written the address. I have a strong feeling its one at the top end of the road, as there are two or three here with small bay windows, and little front gardens, and that accords with my memory of the photos. My dad would have walked around here. I realise I don't even know for certain whether he grew up here, or whether his parents moved here after he left home, and he visited on leave. But he did at least visit, I know that, so I know he has to have walked round these streets. Maybe he arrived home on leave and walked up this street on an evening like this, as I'm doing now.

The house in this street is also part of my own early history. I know we visited and stayed as a family when I was little. My very earliest memory is of staying here, and the excitement generated in me at the unusual bed I was given to sleep in: two armchairs pushed together. This was, I have worked out in conjunction with my mother, when I was about two, before we were posted to Malta, where my brother was born in 1955. I am interested to realise that I am at the site of a personal memory that is over fifty years old.

I explore the surroundings a little more. The houses in the street are not one long terrace, but broken up into sections, built to slightly different designs. Current and recent owners have improved them in the usual variety of ways so that they appear as more of an individualised hotchpotch. Cars and vans are parked in the street, and the odd camper van is apparent. In an adjoining street there are a few thirties semis. Nearby are garages, bits of odd waste land, and alleys and footpaths that lead in and out of the houses.

I am satisfied with my exploration, but frustrated at not knowing the exact house. I search my pockets and wallet carefully, but no, the relevant scrap of paper is not there. I feel temporarily foolish again, at not having brought something so obviously necessary, and then decide to phone home in case I've left it somewhere obvious. There is no-one in, so I leave a message, and head off towards the city centre in search of something to eat.

My phone rings, and I pull in to a little side street away from the traffic. My home support person, Mary, cannot find any sign of the little scrap of paper, but I remember another source for the information and guide her to an old ration book that I have in my possession, now buried deep within a filing cabinet. This reveals the relevant number, and shows that I had been correct in my deductions about which end of the street it was at. Some other information with it reminds me that there was also a sister-in-law of my grandmother's in Ella Street, and her brother in Willerby Road. I can explore them tomorrow.

In the meantime, I head off towards Brunswick Avenue, which I have located on my street map, and which is the site of my dad's secondary school. I know this because amongst our collection of photos and papers is a 1933 copy of 'The Bee', 'The Magazine of the Brunswick Avenue Central Boys' School, Hull.' I have studied this magazine to glean clues as to his history.

In many ways it is a classic school magazine: sports reports, class reports, poems, articles by boys describing for example a trip to London, some creative writing, an editorial, and even an article in French. The tone tends to the humorous (puns and jokes) mixed with moral encouragement.

One of the interesting features to me is that the class reports show only four years. There is no fifth, or sixth form: this is not a grammar school. This is the era when most boys left school at fifteen. In fact there is an emphasis on going out into the world and getting work. The report for 4c says:

'In spite of business depression and consequent cutting down of staffs, the members of the Fourth Form are gradually securing posts. This is evidenced by our numbers, which have been reduced to less than one half since the beginning of the summer term.'

An article about going for an interview for an office job begins: 'A smart looking boy arrived at school the other day, and, contrary to his usual habits, his hair was brushed to brilliance with the contents of the Vaseline jar.'

But others are aiming for something less sedentary: 'To reach the standard measurements required by the Services and the Police Force, four of our form have been doing intensive gymnasium exercises. They must not overlook the fact that brawn alone will not lead to promotion; brawn, more than ever, is taking second place to brain.'

And of particular interest to me in relation to my father:

'One of our number, who is joining the Navy, is likely to start his career on H.M.S. "Ganges." In times of difficulty he should bear in mind his predecessor, H.C., who served on the same ship and overcame difficulties similar to those P.W. will probably meet.'

HMS Ganges is the route into the navy that my dad took three or four years later. It seems clear therefore that there was a tradition of some kind at his school of boys joining the navy, and some kind of support from teachers to enable them to do so. Even if it was only to warn them of the 'times of difficulty' that they would face. I wonder what kind of reality the phrase glosses over. Fifteen or sixteen still seems to me very young to leave home.

My dad (aged twelve at this time) gets a couple of mentions in the magazine. In the report for the football 'C' team: 'In the vanguard Dunn and Armstrong have proved themselves real footballers, not only with regard to the numbers of goals they have scored, but with their conception of the duties of a real footballer, namely, positional play.'

The record of the team ('Captain E. Craig, [2B]. Trainers: Messrs Smethurst and Walker') is phenomenal:

Played	16
Won	16
Lost	0
Drawn	0
Goals for	176
Goals against	4

This is the stuff that schoolboy dreams are made of. Furthermore, in the report for Form 1c is the following: 'The "C" team started the football season with six players from our form. This number is now reduced to three. How is this? Young Armstrong has scored fifty-eight goals. All honour to him. Hayton and Malham have also played well.'

Fifty-eight goals. That's an average of nearly four goals per game, over sixteen games. All honour to him indeed!

From contemplation and enjoyment of his success, I slip easily and familiarly into regret. I never had the chance to talk to him about his exploits. He never had the chance to enjoy the sporting activities that my brother and I engaged in. My brother was sports mad, and played football for the county, as well as football, rugby and cricket for the school, and rugby for his university. I was mad on rugby, and played for the school, played for the Old Boys first team (they ran three or four sides) while still at school, and played for my college. I won events at the district athletics, and went to the county sports. He would have liked that, and been proud of us – and he might also have helped us improve. I always wanted to do better, and be better, but I didn't know how. I tried hard, by doing, for example, my own circuit training in the back garden, but the level of expert input from outside, of any good personal coaching, was minimal. I always have a sense of regret that I didn't really realise my potential. My image of myself at this time is of being rudderless, and therefore, wasteful of progress. Some small guidance on the tiller would have made a big difference.

I have found my way to the location of Brunswick Avenue. There is a large building still there, brick built, two-storeyed, imposing. It could be the school, although it is now a youth centre, and a Primary Care Trust office block. There's no obvious way to find out more, so I just stare at it for a while, and wonder.

It's got dark and I'm feeling tired and I'm getting hungry, and so I head off looking for a suitable eating venue. I come to a MacDonald's. This is not the kind of establishment that someone with my value systems normally enters but tonight it has three advantages: I can lock my bike up to the convenient cycle rack and sit inside where I can still see it; I can order something quick and non-meaty even if its only fries and salad; it's here right now, and I don't have to think any more. I act decisive, and I go in.

Mermaids

Early on a sunny morning, I mingle with Hull folk as they head off on their daily rounds. I see cars, and students, and school children with their bags and their shouts at each other, and shops opening up their shutters for trade. It's all really busy, and purposeful, and what's really wonderful is that I'm not part of it. Instead I'm heading out of town eastwards, but before I leave Hull I'm going to have another wander around my dad's old stamping grounds.

I am feeling good. I have successfully negotiated breakfast. Arriving in the dining room after the builders have gone, I find the landlady in chatty mood with just a couple of her regulars left. She asks me what I'd like cooked, and, remembering the discomfort of Selbyville ('never heard of that before') I come out with a crass phrase like, 'have you got something light?' This is meant to be a subtle code for 'I don't eat meat,' without actually saying, 'I don't eat meat.' The landlady looks at me with a puzzled expression for a few seconds and then breaks the code; 'Are you a vegetarian?' she asks. 'Yes,' I reply. 'And please don't say it so loud,' I think, while to my surprise she offers me beans, toast and Quorn bacon. Then I remember. The reason I wrote down the phone number of this place during my internet searches was because it did vegetarian breakfasts.

I join in conversation with the lady at another table. She is staying here while her trained dog features in a performance at a local theatre. I am impressed. We discuss the kind of life she leads staying in different locations depending on her dog's work schedule, and the fact that the performances are mostly in the evenings, leaving her the daytimes free for exploration.

My own exploration takes me first to Ella Street. This is where my dad's aunt lived, and is only a ten minute walk from where my grandparents lived. This is the area that my dad would have been familiar with as a child and as an adult. Ella Street is a long straight road, tree-lined, with rows of slightly superior terraced houses: they have bay windows, and small front gardens. At intervals small off-shoots, with names like 'The Limes', provide idyllic looking little residential havens: ten terraced houses facing each other across small green gardens, with an access path up the middle.

Round the corner in Salisbury Street, I come across an extraordinary sight. One of the trees in the avenue of trees in this road has died off, and instead of being chopped down, the stump, lopped off at about ten feet above the ground, has been carved into a mermaid. The mermaid is serene of face; she is bare-breasted in traditional style, with prolific tresses of knotted hair, and a long fishy tail. Alongside the mermaid, in runic style capital letters, has been carved the following message: 'I am the mermaid. Look on me as your friend; guiding your long journey till your boat rests at the end.'

I stare round me at the terraced houses, and the gardens, and the grass verges, and the parked cars of this quiet urban street, (Salisbury Street is in fact a few notches up the social scale from Ella Street) and this carving does not fit. It does not compute. There is a dissonance. Or maybe there are more depths to the good people of Hull than I'm tending to give them credit for.

I like the carving very much. I like the message also, which moves me, pulling together as it does themes of the sea, guidance, and life's journey which matter to me. Add to that the smidgeon of unrequitable sexual interest that mermaids carry and you have a powerful brew. And here it is on my dad's childhood territory.

In an even more upmarket area of Hull a little further on, the mermaid theme is continued. In the middle of a quiet road junction, a large ornate structure, perhaps originally a fountain, but now a receptacle for various plants, stands anonymously. It looks like it may date, at a guess, from the twenties. Round the bottom, half hidden by little shrubs, a series of stone mermaids rest on their tails, leaning right back so that their breasts stick up into the air while, with both hands, they hold large elongated shells to their mouths, and, I presume, blow on them.

I investigate Aisne Street again, and look more closely at the house where my dad lived. Unlike in Leeds, there is no convenient resident in the garden to speak to, and I have no inclination to enquire further. I am happy to wander about a little and take in the atmosphere. After a while I head off into town again. On the way, I explore further around the building that may be Brunswick Avenue School. Extensive housing redevelopment has taken place nearby, so that the environment during my dad's time would have been very different.

Passing through the city centre I arrive at the docks area. The Spurn lightship is tied up there, its workaday black paint and clumsy shape at odds with the sleek fripperies of the yachts in the marina. A launch is moored there too, P164, bristling with aerials and equipment of official kinds. I wonder how often my dad came down here, perhaps to be intrigued and inspired, as I am now, by these travellers from other realms. Here, in a real sense, is a gateway to the wider world beyond. Board one of these vessels, cast off, and go anywhere.

My own, less expansive travels take me around the corner, where, on a shady, quiet part of the waterfront, I discover an ancient gent's convenience. Entering there I find, amongst the usual facilities, a wonderland of gleaming polished copper pipes, spotless coloured tiles and ceramic bricks, and a profusion of plants and flowers. Staring in wonder, I think about taking a photo, but another man enters to make use of the facilities, and taking a photograph at this point becomes a less than discreet prospect. Still, my dad and I might have enjoyed seeing this place together: 'I often came here after a few pints with my mates, but it wasn't like this then, I can tell you.'

Railway line

Onward now: past the confluence of the river Hull with the Humber; past the old warehouses backing on to the Hull - once they were the mercantile heart of the town; over the Hull at Drypool Bridge; on through more streets of terraced houses; out past modern estates; past wasteland and urban dereliction, where amongst other graffiti artists, Baz has announced his existence to the world; on to the old railway line that is now my route from Hull towards the coast.

I pause, as the day has got hotter, and I want to remove layers of clothing. An old cyclist passes me. The surface of the track here is good tarmac, and I have no worries. I feel a strange sense of calm as I realise that I have achieved a long-held ambition: I have visited Hull, and explored my dad's childhood home territory. I am on the last leg of my journey. I am going back to my beginnings.

As I make further progress eastwards, the tarmac gives way to cinders, and the broad sweep of the route dwindles to two or three narrow ruts between hawthorn trees and elder trees hung with berries. The cinders, and the flatness of the route, emphasise the railway origins of this cycle track. This is the route of the railway line between Hull and Withernsea, on the coast.

On this railway, in about 1949, my mother and a friend of hers came out one evening to go to a dance in Withernsea. She met my dad there. That's where it started. You could say that's where I started. She has told me the story. This is it.

"My friend and I saw a poster advertising a dance in Withernsea. It was at the Palace, I think. We didn't normally go out there for dances, but we thought it might be fun to do something different. We caught the train. When we got there, we sat down with a drink and looked around. My friend said, 'Look over there - there's a smashing looking man in a naval uniform.' Well he came over and asked me to dance. He was a good dancer, and we had several dances together, and I liked him at once. He was called Ernie. It turned out that there was a competition of some kind that needed judging, and one of the judges hadn't turned up. They'd asked Ernie if he would do it, probably because he was wearing uniform. When they called him up on the loudspeaker, I got a shock because he had the same surname as mine – Armstrong. When it came time to go, my friend and I got in the carriage in the train. Then I saw your dad, with his friend, coming up the train looking in all the carriages. When they got to mine they got in, and we started chatting. He turned to me and starting saying, 'Before we go any further, I...' And I interrupted, very quick, 'Who's saying we're going to go any further?' But of course, I did want to see him, and we agreed to meet for a drink the next night, and it just went on from there."

The track goes past an old station, now converted to a house, with the platform still there, the old concrete flaking under the passing years. Strange to think that early on that evening they both came down this line, possibly on the same train, as single people, and later that night went back to Hull together on this same line, and were a couple from then on. They must have seen this station. They would have been having those early falling-in-love conversations as the train paused here on the return journey.

After negotiating a stretch of track which tractors have been using, creating enormous ruts and spectacular potholes, I stop for a mid-day break by a large deep drainage channel. In front of me are two fields, one ploughed, and one ploughed and harrowed, with the neat lines left by the discs swooping round the field in regular parallel lines. Beyond, a windmill on the near skyline testifies to the remnants of times past. In the hot autumn sunshine, a red butterfly alights on a single remaining late dandelion. A beautiful grey-blue dragonfly zips here and there around me. Huge sloes hang in the hedgerow, alongside ripe elderberries. That familiar autumnal smell of rot, and decay, wafts faintly on the breeze.

My phone rings, and it is Baz. He is the friend who has agreed to meet me in Withernsea, and take me and my bike back to his home in York. It is another reminder of journey's end closing in. I'm reluctant to acknowledge this. The journey, time out of normal life, has become familiar and precious to me, and I don't want to face the next transition. But Baz's usual cheery voice is practical and curious. He wants to know where I am, and how far I've got. I tell him I'm on the old railway line, about half way to Withernsea.

"Oh, I know that line. I've travelled on it loads." Baz grew up in Withernsea, and is going to show me round. "We used to travel into Hull on it all the time when I was a kid. Till Dr Beeching axed it in – what was it? – 1966? Hey, it'll be good to cycle on, at least it's flat. You could cycle all the way into Withernsea on that. Just keep going."

We agree to meet in Withernsea, 'by the twin towers', in a couple of hours. I pack up, and set off again.

My parents' courtship, as I understand it, lasted a couple of years. It must have been hard on them, as my dad was away all the time, and only home on leave. My mother has talked about her excitement when she knew he was coming back, and how she would go to the station to meet him, and catch that first, long-awaited glimpse. Like all separated people of that era, their communication was by letter. Later, when they were married, if they had to be apart, they would often write every day. I expect that their letters during their courtship were also frequent.

The line comes to another station, again converted to someone's home. But here the trackbed has been filled in and become a driveway. Across this is a large gate, and upon the gate hangs a large sign. This bears the words, in suitably large letters, 'Private Property'. I stare beyond the gate at the neat suburban lawns and shrubs now filling the space where porters might have lounged, and parcels and luggage been stacked waiting for the next train to puff its way in. No doubt many other couples besides my parents might have found fond recollections waiting for them here.

I find the alternative route round, and re-join the line. As I have got further from the city, the cycleway available to me has gradually diminished. I imagine hordes of cyclists setting off with gay abandon and enthusiasm, and one by one turning back as their energy flags. It seems I am now in territory reached only by the hardy few, for the cinder path available to me between the long grass on each side has shrunk to six inches wide. This, as we know, is sufficient for we cyclists, but I fear that time, and the line, is running out for me also. At the next road crossing, where a single short length of iron rail sticks out a little forlornly from the ground, my cinders come to an end. The track continues on the other side, but the way is entirely covered in thick undergrowth. I admit defeat, and take myself, once more, out on to the public highway.

A decision has to be made. For a habitual fence-sitter such as myself, this is a difficult moment. I can go right, hit the main road in a short distance, and investigate the railway line at a couple of places further on. The map seems to show a track leading down to Withernsea itself. Or I can go left, and stick with minor roads for a while before hitting a brown 'B' road that will bring me to Withernsea. The possibility of the railway line being useable further on seems dubious, and if it isn't useable, then I'm committed to the main road. About seven miles' worth of main road, no doubt streaming with white van men, and their assorted friends. I play safe, and go left along minor roads.

Dog legs in the road bring me occasionally into conflict with the prevailing westerlies. They are still powerful, and require me to drop down several gears to maintain momentum, even on these flat lands. I come to the B road by a pub. I don't like the look of it. It's busy. I study the map and decide to make a detour along further minor roads. It will be three miles of yellow roads to avoid a mile and a half of brown road. A bargain! In Zen terms, I will continue to enjoy the journey, and the destination will remain the enjoyment of the journey.

The enjoyment includes a dead rat on the road, my first of the journey. The rat provides the fourth dead species that I recall, joining pheasants, hedgehogs, and squirrels. Several pheasants, happily very much alive, crowd their way through a hedge a short distance ahead of my progress.

I leave hedges behind, and enter a world of enormous flat ploughed and harrowed fields, on either side of the road, stretching away to the horizon. At my feet a bit of black tarmac, then a small green verge, then the huge acreage of brown, then the sky of blue. Above my head, and all around, the sky of blue, with white clouds dotted about in endlessly changing patterns. Then the opposite horizon, the expanse of brown soil, and the short green verge on the other side of the road, and back to the tarmac at my feet.

I am alone with the wind in this wide and open world. My way divides two huge fields, one from the other. They rest peacefully, and solidly, on either side of me. I thread my way between them.

My parents married in the summer of 1951. By this time, Dot and Jim had moved to Leeds, and so my parents were married from their house in Crossgates, a Leeds suburb. After a honeymoon sailing in the Broads, they settled to married life in Ipswich. My dad was back at HMS Ganges, working this time as one of the instructors. From what my mum has said, and from entries in a joint diary that they kept, it is clear that in these early days of married life they were intensely happy. They were living in a small rented flat. Sometimes my dad came home after work, had his tea, and then had to go back to the base, sometimes for the night. After a very short space of time as a stay-at-home wife, my mother got a part-time job working in the office of a cinema. At weekends, they made each other cups of tea in bed, went for walks, or went to the cinema. My mother kept up a frequent correspondence with her sister Mary, with Dot and Jim, with her father, with Miss Sunley, her old landlady from Helmsley, with Aunt Sally, her old foster mother, and with others.

Within the year, my dad had been transferred to Portsmouth. He went there first so that he could find lodgings suitable to accommodate a pregnant wife, and expected child. My mother has told me that when they got married, she said to my dad, 'Let's not wait, let's try for a baby straight away.' And they didn't wait. In the first flush of their sexual love for each other, while they were young, and fresh, and beautiful, and handsome, they created a space of love and passion, and there conceived a child. In Portsmouth, in the summer of 1952, a year after they married, the baby was born.

The christening followed on within a few weeks. I know this because it is well documented by small black and white photographs taken in the back garden. I am there, the small baby in white christening clothes. My parents hold me between them. My dad, with his short-back-and–sides brylcreemed hair, is wearing his double-breasted suit with wide trousers. My mother wears a floral dress, and looks radiant. I am held up between them with their loving faces close alongside mine.

The ploughed and harrowed fields on either side of me come to an end. I turn on to the 'B' road. A short distance along it is a sign marking the Greenwich meridian: 0 degrees, with an arrow pointing east, and another pointing west. I pause and contemplate it. Perhaps it has some kind of added significance? Perhaps it could be linked to the equinox, another point of equilibrium. But no, it's just an artificial number after all. They could have decided to allocate it anywhere.

As I come into the town, I go past the striking white lighthouse towering above the houses incongruously surrounding it. Withernsea is here faster than I can comprehend. All is change, nothing is permanent, I know, but I'm still trying to hang on to my journey, and my journey is fast slipping from my grasp. I would like to wander at ease round this new place, explore it at my own idiosyncratic pace, and let it seep into me. I would like to ponder on the journey that's been, and think about my mum and dad, and their meeting here. There may be more insights to gain, more understanding to be had.

I had tried to arrange it so I arrived well before Baz and would only meet up with him when I was ready, when I'd digested what needed digesting. But Baz, bless him, has left work early, arrived early, and I bump into his cheery presence as soon as I hit the main street. Very Baz. Ready or not, my solitary journey is over.

Baz immediately sets us off on a tour of his home town. I'm caught up in family history – but someone else's this time. Baz grew up here. We go past the site of the fairground where he got his first job, aged 10, putting the ducks back in the water for the lucky dip. We go past an extraordinary outside stage, with full concrete canopy, set in some recently recreated gardens. Baz tells me this commemorates a childhood friend of his, Dave, who used to organise festivals here, and died recently. I suggest to Baz that he might like to appear on the stage. He does not take a lot of persuading, and, centre-stage, he demonstrates dramatic air guitar, before modestly acknowledging the adulation of the non-assembled multitudes.

I interview him as we walk on, round his childhood haunts. Baz still has a great local accent, despite living away all his adult life, but, a born performer, he can turn his hand to posh, or Welsh, as occasion demands.

'So, Barry, has your family always lived in Withernsea?'

'No, Peter; my dad came here from Hull with his dad. My grandfather came and set up an ice cream business. Later on my dad ran a kind of men's club, near the sea front. I'll take you past it. The building's still there. It was a place where they could hang out and be sociable.'

'What about your mum? Did she grow up here?'

'No, she came from London. She was a nurse and came up here on holiday with a friend, met my dad, and they fell in love.'

'I believe they met at a dance hall.'

'That's correct, Peter. The Palace in Withernsea.'

'By a strange coincidence, the same dance hall where my mum met my dad.'

'It is a very strange coincidence, as I believe we have discussed before.'

'And round about the same historical era, in fact – in the late forties.'

'Correct.'

'Perhaps even at the same dance?'

'I think that would be pushing things too far, don't you?'

'Probably it would, Barry. So your mum moved up here to live?'

'Yes, when they got married. Recently I found some of the letters they wrote when they were engaged. They're very passionate and tender. They want to get married as soon as possible. They're both saying they can't wait. He's always pressing her to get married.'

'My mum and dad seem to have written more or less every day when they were apart, before they got married. She'd fret if there wasn't a letter from him. Sometimes the post would be delayed, and then she'd get two or three letters at once. It's all a bit different from our day. Pre-phones. My mum used to write letters to her future mother-in-law, and they were both living in Hull.'

We reach the sea. We pause and I lean my bike against the sea wall. Then we both lean on the sea wall as well. The sea is grey and wild, and churned up. The wind is still blowing strongly, and I keep my hands in my jacket pockets.

'And after they were married, they continued to live in Withernsea?'

'Right the way through. My mum died last year. She'd lived in the same council house from when it was new, fifty years ago. I'll show you – I'll take you past it.'

'And your dad?'

'Died in his seventies, maybe about ten years ago.'

Further along the sea wall we pass the old club that Baz's dad used to run. We pass the pond where Baz and his mates used to fish. We pass an older man.

'Did you see him?' Baz hisses at me when we are safely past.

'Yes, what about him?' I hiss back.

'That's the Withernsea intellectual.'

'That's the Withernsea intellectual? Is there only one?'

'There was only one when I was a lad. He read The Guardian, and had left wing views, and smoked dope. We all knew him.'

'Wasn't he lonely – being the only one?

'Wouldn't you be? In Withernsea! I got out, he's still here.'

We turn away from the front, and then turn again and head back towards the town. I'm still pushing my bike with all its gear on. We've walked a long way, and it's quite hard work to keep it upright, and at the same time avoid ankle-banging painfulness. We turn into a small quiet housing estate.

'We'll just see if she's in,' says Baz, going up to a door and ringing the bell. I wait on the pavement to see what happens next in my life.

A woman answers the door, and there are excited exclamations and greetings of a muted kind. Baz waves in my direction and introduces me.

'This is a mate of mine, Pete, he's on a cycling trip and he's ended up in Withernsea. So I've come to meet him and give him a lift back. This is my cousin Belinda.' We smile and say hello. Baz and I get invited in for a cup of tea. I lock up my bike and follow them into a small living room. This is jammed with stuff, including many jigsaws, some finished and some not. Space is made for us and we sit down. I'm introduced to Jack, Belinda's husband. We get tea and biscuits. Baz and Belinda and Jack engage in an intense exchange of news and views on family matters. I learn that Baz's sister is in South Africa, and Belinda's sister is in California. There is discussion of children, and who is with who, and who is living where. There is discussion of the facilities that the local council provide for Belinda and Jack's daughter, who has a disability. There are anecdotes from the past, and reminiscences of people now dead.

I feel very much the outsider, the observer. I cannot take part in most of this conversation, and they don't try to include me. I am content to accept this as part of the journey. It is intense family stuff, and it is familiar to me – the love, the interest, the laughter, the criticism, the shared experiences and history. Only the details are different – it is their family, not mine. I feel like I did as a child when I was taken round to see relatives that I didn't know. I have almost no control in the situation, and have to accept what is. It is good practice, in the Buddhist sense.

Baz decides it's time for us to go, and we head off. We pass the council house he grew up in, just across the way from Belinda's. We pass the old people's home where Baz's mother lived and died. We pass a second-hand shop that Baz used to patronise. As dusk descends, we pass a guy in the street, and Baz stops to chat. He was the drummer in Baz's band. Baz went away, he's still here. I'm still feeling like a child – excluded from the stuff that adults like talking about, and a little bit bored as a consequence.

I'm standing slightly apart from Baz and the drummer, holding my bike still by putting the brakes on, when one of the brakes malfunctions. One of the toggles at the end of the brake cable has come out of its housing. It's not serious, just fiddly to put right, and I leave it till later. My journey is over. I don't need my bike any more.

We walk on to where Baz has parked his car. It's at the Pavilion, a modern building which, according to Baz, is on the site of the original dance hall where both our sets of parents met. We both stare at it for a while. You could say we both started here.

We don't say anything. We take my gear off the bike and put it in the car. I take the wheels off the bike, and we fit it in the back of the car. My bike and I have finished our journey. It's over.

Postscript

Sometime after the journey ended, I picked up the phone one day, and the voice on the other end said, 'It's Leo.' There was a slight pause, and then he said, 'Baz is dead.' He said it very evenly, with a slight tone of wonderment in his voice.

Oddly, I felt little surprise – sometimes I don't feel much surprise, or upset, when I hear that people I know are dead. In a strange way, I'm kind of expecting them to be dead, and to be hearing the news that they're dead. Perhaps I learned to respond in this way as a child, so that I could protect myself a little from the kind of shock which had already happened to me, a shock which, I realised, could therefore happen again. On hearing the news about Baz, as with others, I had the thought 'Ah, so it was Baz who was next. I wonder who'll come after?'

Leo and Baz had been friends since they met in Luton when Baz first left Withernsea.

'So what's happened?'

'Baz came home from work. He said he felt tired and had a few pains in his arms. He went upstairs to lie down on the bed. Later on Jo went upstairs and found him dead. It was probably his heart, but we don't know.'

I thought of Baz. He was not far short of his fifty-fifth birthday, and had been planning retirement from his work as a psychiatric nurse. His pension was due. He was really looking forward to a new life of relative freedom. He and Jo had been together a long time but had got married only recently. They had a daughter. When my journey ended, Baz had taken me back to his house, and I had stayed there for the night. I had helped Erin with her homework, and it had been fun. She had a lovely sense of fun like her dad. Now she was going to have to manage without him.

Leo and I discussed the funeral. He was going to be heavily involved in helping to organise it. I asked whether I could do anything to help, and we agreed I would phone round our friends and let them have the news. I made several phone calls right away, and got mostly answer machines. Dilemma: to leave the news on the machine, or ask them to ring back as soon as possible? I decided to leave the news on the machines. I warned them that there was some bad news to come, told them what had happened to Baz, and invited them to ring me back if they needed more information.

The funeral took place at a cemetery in York. I arrived early, and decided to explore. It was a big, old, sprawling cemetery, with many lovely mature trees scattered about. I spotted a newly dug grave, and figured it would be the one ready for Baz. I wandered over. I wondered where the grave diggers were, and how long it had taken them to do it. Did they dig it the day before? Such a lot of hard physical work needed to provide someone's last resting place. Did they think about the person who would remain there while they did it? It would have been better if we, his friends, could have dug it. Dug it with awareness of him: remembering him, reminiscing about him. I approached the grave. It had the usual sheets of bright green imitation grass laid over the mounds of earth next to it. Mental note to myself: leave clear instructions for no imitation grass at my grave. Good old brown earth for me. I looked down into the grave. I was taken aback to see a coffin already there.

I realised there must have been a funeral already, earlier in the morning. But how could the coffin just be left here? I looked around. There was no-one in sight. I was the only person taking any notice of this anonymous body, alone in the bottom of the grave. It didn't feel right. No doubt the grave diggers were planning to come back later and fill the grave in, but at this moment, I felt an air of loneliness and vulnerability hanging around the coffin. The funeral had taken place, and everyone had been very involved, and then at a certain point, the mourners had simply abandoned their person and gone off to have their tea and sandwiches. It seemed like the job was left unfinished. Of course they were following convention, but it still didn't feel right. There was no-one to keep guard, to keep watch, to keep the faith.

I looked around again. The scene was quiet and peaceful. Greenery, trees, ordered grave stones. Maybe I was creating loneliness and abandonment where only peace and serenity existed. Maybe the dead person was lying at the bottom of the grave, enjoying the final sense of connection with the air and the light before being tucked up in the ground forever. Maybe they were just dead and it didn't matter. Maybe none of it mattered. Here it is. This is simply how it is.

Further away, in a secluded spot amongst some trees, I found another freshly dug grave. There was more imitation grass. There was no coffin.

I was still early, and I waited near to the ornate Victorian building in the middle, where the funeral would be held. The doors were open, and the room inside was being prepared by some of Baz's York friends that I didn't know. There were chairs being put out, and flowers arranged, and a sound system being set up.

Gradually more people arrived, including my particular group of friends, of which Baz had been a member. Leo was up front, sorting out details with others, getting ready to speak, getting ready to manage the ceremony.

Finally Baz arrived, carried in a wicker coffin, placed at the front. The lid came off, and he was there, dressed in a long white gown, his greying hair swept back from his face.

The room was full, but more people arrived and squeezed in at the sides and the back. Others stood at the open doors at the back, and others stood behind them. There was quite a crowd who took part in the funeral from outside. Baz knew a lot of people.

Leo did a difficult job very beautifully. He held the space so that the rest of us - family, friends, fellow musicians, people from work - could make contributions. There were readings, and anecdotes, and music, and heartfelt grief. We were sad, we cried, we laughed, we were solemn.

Leo said afterwards, 'I was emotionally exhausted, battered. But I knew it was an important job, and I wanted to do for Jo, make it the way she wanted it. My regret is that I didn't have anything much left to say about Baz myself.'

Leo and Malcolm, Eric and Nick, Dafydd, Ewan and I stood at the front and sang a song to say goodbye to Baz. He had been part of our group, bringing his extraordinary energy and cheeriness, and his songs and guitar playing. Now we stood in a line behind his coffin, facing the other people and sang 'The Connemara cradle song' a lullaby that formed part of our repertoire when we met together. We had sung it together on many occasions. At one point we held hands. I was on the end of the line, next to Baz's feet. I reached out and held his toe, joining him to us one last time. His toe was cold.

On the wings of the wind o'er the dark rolling deep

Angels are coming to watch o'er thy sleep
Angels are coming to watch o'er thee
So list to the wind coming over the sea

Chorus:
Hear the wind blow, dear
Hear the wind blow
Lean your head over
And hear the wind blow

The currachs are sailing way out in the blue
Laden with herring of silvery hue
Silver the herring and silver the sea
And soon there'll be silver for baby and me

The currachs tomorrow will stand on the shore
And daddy goes sailing, a-sailing no more
The nets will be drying, the nets heaven blessed
And safe in my arms, dear, contented he'll rest

Leo's partner Anna has said that she had been holding it together up to that point, but when she heard this beautiful song, and saw us all standing there, that was the point at which she had to let go, and let grief take over.

Later on, after the planned offerings, Leo had invited contributions from anyone else present who felt they had something to offer. Towards the end of this period, there were occasional gaps, as people contemplated, and wondered whether there was anyone else with something to say. We had been meeting together for a good while. There were no artificial constraints imposed on us by the demands of a service. No queue of mourners for the next funeral standing outside the crematorium, waiting for our allotted twenty minutes to end, so that we could file out and they could file in. We were taking as long as it needed. Already at this funeral, I felt we had done more justice to Baz, and to his life, than at any other I had been to.

In one of the gaps I felt tempted to offer a song, 'No coming, no going.' The words for this song are adapted from a piece - Contemplation on No-coming, No-going - composed by Thich Nhat Hanh. He took the words and teachings from the sutra to be 'Given to the Dying' in the Anguttara Nikaya. Thich Nhat Hanh wrote his piece as a lullaby that can be sung to those who need comfort in the presence of death. I had set the words to a lullaby tune that emerged one time with the Gaffers.

I could feel my heart beating a little faster as I contemplated the prospect. It would mean going to the front, borrowing a guitar that was there, explaining a little bit about it, and then singing. I was worried that I might mess up, or forget the words. However, the really difficult question was to decide whether it was right for this moment. It might be more about me than about Baz, or about the needs of the community that was meeting at this moment. How do you tell?

We'd created a special place, where authentic truth and love were able to be spoken and heard. In those circumstances, everyone's choices contribute to the collective centre of gravity, and help to elevate or depress the atmosphere. The really difficult thing in deciding whether to contribute is that there is really no hiding place. If you go in with something, and your ego is heavily involved, it will bring the atmosphere down. However, if you have something that really needs to be said, and you sit on it, you will also bring down the atmosphere. Unfortunately the ego is heavily involved in false modesty also. No escape! You've got to make your call and live with the consequences. Be as precise as you can, be courageous, pay attention to your feelings, check out for undue ego involvement, and then if you do go for it, watch for feedback as you go along.

In the event, someone else filled the gap, the moment passed, and I breathed a sigh of relief – I didn't have to decide, I didn't have to put myself forward and sing.

Thich Nhat Hanh's Vietnamese form of Zen Buddhism emphasises the interconnectedness of everything. We are not separate beings in the way we mostly think we are. There is no beginning and no end, but there are transformations.

If I had sung, these are the words that would have been heard:

> This body's not me; I'm not caught in this body.
> I am life untied, never been born and never died.
> Look up at the stars filling the sky, look at the ocean wide,
> Manifestations from my wondrous true mind.

> Since beginningless time I have always been free.
> Birth and death are a game, a game of hide-and-seek
> Birth and death are doors, doors through which we pass,
> Sacred thresholds on our myriad paths.

> So smile to me, take my hand, wave goodbye,
> We shall meet again, oh tomorrow, or maybe today
> We shall always be meeting again at the true source,
> Always meeting again in life in all its forms.

At Baz's funeral, we followed the coffin as we processed through the graveyard. We sang 'As I went down in the river to pray,' till we reached the graveside. We gathered round. The coffin was lowered in. Some final words were said, some final flowers thrown in the grave with him. People started to drift away.

I'd seen two or three shovels leaning against a tree nearby. I spoke to some of the others about maybe filling in the grave, and we had little quiet discussions, and hung about waiting. We would see what opportunities there were. I didn't want Baz to be left unattended in his coffin at the bottom of the grave.

We spotted one of the cemetery people at the back of the dwindling crowd and we approached her. We told her we were interested in filling in the grave. She was a young woman and she was non-committal at first.

'It's a bit difficult,' she said. 'It's better if I get my grave diggers to do it.'

'What's difficult?' we said. 'We're here, and Baz was our friend. It's something we want to do for him.'

Perhaps by this time she was getting the idea we were serious, and not sentimental.

'I don't mind you doing it,' she said, 'as long as you understand what's involved. It's just that some people get a bit upset when they realise what you have to do.'

'What do you have to do?'

'Well, putting the soil back in is just part of the job. The other part is you have to compact it down. You understand? Otherwise it will just sink over time, and leave a big hollow. Basically you have to get into the grave and jump up and down on the soil to make it compact. That's what gets some people upset.'

We looked around at each other. 'We're OK with that.'

A couple of Baz's other friends joined us. Pretty well everyone else had gone by now. We removed the plastic grass, got the tools, and we set to. The young woman watched to check things were going as they should.

The first few shovelfuls of soil rained in. When there was a good layer of soil down there, someone got in the grave and started treading the soil down and jumping on it. Whichever end he was at, we threw soil in at the other one. After a while we would change ends to even things up. We took turns. We swapped roles, we took rests. It wasn't upsetting. It was good, careful, satisfying work. We put him to rest.

I think Baz would have approved. I imagine him laughing, and cracking jokes about us finally dancing on his grave. In fact dancing in his grave. I imagine him strumming his guitar in his usual energetic way and singing to us as we went about our work. One of his trademark songs, along with 'Black Jack Davy' and 'Log Cabin in the Sky' was a strange, jolly, country-style number, usually sung in a fake southern country-boy accent:

> By the marks (by the marks) where the nails have been,
> By the signs (by the signs) on his precious skin,
> I will know my Saviour when I come to him,
> By the marks where the nails have been.

Afterwards Leo said: "It was important to shape it ourselves as much as possible. You can't let the professionals do too much. He was our friend.

"There was so much to organise. We wanted to have candles in the room we used at the cemetery, but they wouldn't let us. Health and safety of course. I just said to myself, 'Don't stick on it, don't stick on it. Let it go.' And we moved on.

"Baz was such a cheerful bugger. He was so light-hearted all the time. He came down to Luton and got a shit job in a petrol station on the M1. But he didn't care. He'd come home with a raft of funny stories and jokes about work each night.

"He showed me how you didn't have to be afraid of the world. You could just go out and play in it and have a great time, a fun time."

Maybe we can all learn to go out there and play in the world and have a great time, a fun time.

Keep playing Baz. Keep playing.

Afterword

Thanks for reading this far and I hope you have found the book both enjoyable and useful.

You'll find more information about my other books on the holybloke website (holybloke.com).

On the website also you can find some photos from the ride and from my early years (http://www.holybloke.com/books/riding-into-the-storm-pics/).

You can also become a holybloke follower and receive email alerts when new poems, posts, and books are published. Sign up on the website.

Finally, if you have enjoyed the book, please could you consider leaving a short review on Amazon? Help other people to find it and enjoy it too!

Also available

Pete's first book of poems, ***The Commitment of the Lark: poems for looking deeply*** received this review:

'These poems are remarkably refreshing and invigorating. If you are interested in living life to the full, deeply, honestly, out on the open ocean, away from the safe harbour of dogma, then you will find this book very nourishing. Pete Armstrong's writing has an incisive vitality, a warmth, a curiosity, a compassion, humour, a desire to embrace the whole of life's experience including the 'shadow' as well as the numinous (and indeed, to see the numinous within the shadow), exploring a spiritual path that is very much of the here and now, the everyday. If you are interested in Ken Wilber's Integral writings, Buddhism, mystical Christianity, psychology, these poems will surely touch and inspire you.'

The Commitment of the Lark is available from Amazon as a paperback, and also as an e-book for Kindle.

His **second book of poems** is ***Target Practice: a guidebook of 100 poems for your inner journey***

The poems in *Target Practice* are travellers' tales from an inner journey. They contain insights, tips on how to travel safely, and on dangers to avoid.
These poems tell of the experiences and insights of exploration, both inner and outer.
They emerge in and through meditation, and the clarity that can come as part of that. Some are like jokes, and should make you laugh, or at least smile.
Target practice is like a guidebook for your journey into your unknown future.

Target Practice is available as a paperback on Amazon and as an e-book for Kindle.

Coming soon

Fifty-fifty: an inner journey through the Lakes
An account of a walk through the English Lake District with the theme of the transition into being an older man.

How to write poems from a deeper place: meditation, poetry and inner work
A comprehensive guide to writing your own poems from a place of meditation and clarity.

Printed in Great Britain
by Amazon.co.uk, Ltd.,
Marston Gate.